The Goodness Campaign

getting back to good

ken ferrara

authorHOUSE®

AuthorHouse™
1663 Liberty Drive
Bloomington, IN 47403
www.authorhouse.com
Phone: 1-800-839-8640

Published by AuthorHouse 1/3/2012

ISBN: 978-1-4685-0622-8 (sc)
ISBN: 978-1-4685-0621-1 (e)

Printed in the United States of America

Any people depicted in stock imagery provided by Thinkstock are models, and such images are being used for illustrative purposes only. Certain stock imagery © Thinkstock.

This book is printed on acid-free paper.

You have the power to
improve everything in your life.

Will you harness it?

Opportunities to enhance your health, improve your relationships, and bring you happiness, peace, and fulfillment will cross your path every day. Perhaps most important of all, those opportunities can empower you to make a difference; in your life…and in the world. Will you grasp them?

the essence of a new day

This is the beginning of a new day. You have been given this day to use as you will. You can waste it or use it for good. What you do today is important because you are exchanging a day of your life for it. When tomorrow comes, this day will be gone forever; in its place is something you have left behind... let it be something good.

–Unknown

Welcome...to your
Goodness Campaign

Every choice you make and action you take is important and has the potential to bring powerful, positive changes into your life. From interactions with family and friends, to that person beside you, to the ways you treat your environment and yourself; an incredible potential of goodness exists.

Look closely...

- **Could your health, relationships, and choices be better?**
- **Are you as patient, compassionate, selfless, and generous as possible—with yourself, as well as others?**
- **What would make you happier and more fulfilled?**
- **Are you as successful as you want to be in your endeavors?**
- **Have you dreamed about making a difference in your life...and our world?**

Experience the positive power and energy you can create by choosing to share the goodness that is within your reach every day. Imagine what you could accomplish: becoming healthier, repairing relationships, helping others, restoring balance to your life and environment, and finding lasting fulfillment and happiness...the list goes on and on!

Opportunities appear every second,

don't let another moment pass you by.

Participating in your goodness campaign is an easy way to intentionally grasp those opportunities and do something good for yourself, and just as importantly, for someone else. Consciously making an effort to live with more good thoughts and actions will inspire and encourage you to notice the absolute beauty that surrounds you everyday, and be thankful.

Over time, good gets better!

Once you start your campaign, great things will happen. You'll be stronger, healthier, and feel energized, invigorated, renewed, and happier. Over time, your good actions will create more positive perspectives, opportunities, and outcomes in your life, and improve every life you touch.

"Then, without realizing it, you try to improve yourself at the start of each new day; of course, you achieve quite a lot in the course of time. Anyone can do this; it costs nothing and is certainly very helpful." –Anne Frank

**We cannot edit our past, but we can
correct the present and right (write) our future.**

We, all of us, have made mistakes or not lived up to our full potential at one time or another. These things tarnish relationships, the way we feel about others and ourselves, and can make us live with regret and guilt. Well, consider today a *fresh, blank* page where you grab a newly sharpened pencil and begin writing the rest of your life's story…letting go of what you can from the past, correcting the present, and moving forward with goodness.

**This world is a wonderful,
bountiful home we share, but…**

There seems to be a shift away from goodness—from being as good as we can be…personally, and on a global scale as well. Beliefs indeed vary; values and circumstances may be unique; but ultimately, we share common bonds of hope, love, happiness, and wanting to live a healthy, purposeful life. Living with goodness is essential in order to make these things a bigger part of our lives. You could almost say it is a tie that binds each of us to the other; and one by one we can make a difference by positively focusing on that binding tie.

simple — effective — contagious

Simply share two acts of goodness: one for yourself and one for someone else, then write those down. That's it! Do this for one day and pass it on, and you will be an official participant in the Goodness Campaign! These acts can be as simple as focusing on good, positive thoughts, spending some extra time with a loved one, or sharing a smile. You can have a healthy meal, take a walk, and offer a sincere, heartfelt thank you; volunteer, donate your time and finances, and if your spirit moves you, pray—the sky's the limit!

I know, I know, on the surface this seems too simplistic, too trivial. How can taking a few moments each day to care for yourself and others with small, meaningful thoughts and actions affect any *real* change? The truth is that we can easily become so overwhelmed with everyday life that we may overlook the simple ways we are able to contribute something good...and those things, when added together, develop powerfully and exponentially.

One thought or action of goodness is like a single drop of water... in and of itself, rather insignificant. However, when enough drops come together, water becomes powerfully life sustaining. The same is true with good thoughts and actions...they create mighty waves that weave around our world, sustaining and enhancing everything and everyone they touch. The best part of living with more goodness is that the wave you create ultimately finds its way back to you.

Every good deed done to others is a great force that starts an unending pulsation through time and eternity. We may not know it, we may never hear a word of gratitude or recognition, but it will all come back to us in some form as naturally, as perfectly, as inevitably, as echo answers to sound.

—William George Jordan

The more you give, the better you will be...physically, emotionally, and spiritually. You don't have to do things that are huge or cinematic, simply genuine. I encourage you to jump-start your campaign by participating right now for just one day, and start changing your world!

- **Positive change is in the air.**
- **One thought, one intention, one action.**
- **For yourself, your loved ones, and the world.**

Your Goal = One Day

Remember the question I asked on the first few pages? If you see opportunities to enhance your health and relationships, make you feel happier and live with greater peace of mind, will you grasp them? Well, right now is the perfect time to find out! Find a couple of minutes and a quiet spot; maybe listen to your favorite song, grab a seat in a comfortable chair, and contemplate for a moment on what you can do today to achieve this goal. It will only take a few minutes; you'll be glad you did!

The first part of your campaign will consist of doing something for others; a family member or friend, a person you just met, or someone halfway 'round the world. You can include anything you have done to help nature as well. The world is at your fingertips; just be sincere and from the heart…the ideas will come!

Here are some examples to inspire:
- If getting irritated while driving describes you to a tee, make a conscious effort to stay calm and patient in situations you normally wouldn't.
- Perhaps you'll see a person struggling to carry a bag; offer to help.
- Maybe you can donate some of your time or money.
- Help a friend or say sorry to a loved one.
- Make room for a person to sit next to you on the train, smile and say hi, or pay that toll for the person behind you.
- Hug those close to you and tell them how much you love them—your spouse, children, family, and friends.
- These are just a few examples, what else can you think of?

The second element of your campaign will be to do something good for yourself—eat a healthy meal, exercise, take some time out to relax, say a prayer of thanks, or work on a project or goal you may have been putting off…you decide! Just don't get so caught up in deciding what to do that you don't do anything☺. Remember, these actions can be small or large…they can be fun or something a little more on the serious side (i.e. apologizing or forgiving someone).

Ask yourself these questions…
- Do I treat others with less kindness, patience, and tolerance than I could?

- Do I take care of myself; eating healthy, exercising, lowering the amount of stress I deal with, and finding quality time for those important to me?
- Am I as generous and giving as I should be? As I could be?
- Can I forgive someone and take the first step to make things right?
- What am I taking for granted today?
- What can I do to make my life, someone else's life, or the world better?
- Am I noticing all that I have been blessed with and being truly thankful for it?

Plenty of opportunities to think and act with more goodness are present every day. From talking to a family member or friend you have not spoken with for a while, to simply letting that car pull out in front of you; from living a healthier lifestyle to maintaining a more positive perspective, you can make good choices that will bring immense benefits to you. With the special skills, abilities, opportunities, and choices you have, you can change your life and the lives of those around you for the better! Once you start, many doors will open and positive paths will appear...you'll see!

Sure, from time to time, we are all *less than good*, but those moments harbor the perfect opportunities to make changes for the better. I'm going to ask you to stop reading now and complete a one-day campaign today. Take full advantage of this great chance to find more goodness in your life and make your difference. After you complete your *one-day goodness campaign,* fill in the journal that follows, and continue reading. Have fun with this and learn more about getting back to good.

My Goodness Campaign 1-Day

Date: _____
(circle what applies)

Good For Others: Family / Friends / Nature / Others:

_____
_____
_____
_____
_____
_____
_____
_____
_____
_____

Good for Myself: Mind / Body / Spirit / Financial / Other:

_____
_____
_____
_____
_____
_____
_____
_____
_____
_____

Congratulations! You are improving your life and enhancing our world. How do you feel? What did you achieve? Did you brighten someone's day, take a little better care of yourself, or make that apology you've been putting off? Regardless of what it is, you've started a momentum of goodness here that can grow into something huge and exciting. The more you give…the more will return to you! In order for this campaign to be truly successful, all you have to do is…

to laugh often and much; to win the respect of intelligent people and the affection of children; to earn the appreciation of honest critics and endure the betrayal of a false friend; to appreciate beauty; to find the best in others; to leave the world a bit better; whether by a healthy child, garden patch, or redeemed social condition; to know even one life breathed easier because you have lived. This is to have succeeded.

-Ralph Waldo Emerson

The Goodness Campaign starts with one day…but doesn't end there; goodness needs to be encouraged and nurtured daily, and this campaign is an excellent tool to help you do just that! If you like what you've felt and accomplished so far, and want to keep welcoming better health and relationships into your life; making better choices, experiencing more positive attitudes and outcomes, and finding more happiness, gratitude, and fulfillment, then I encourage you to continue reading and commit to make this campaign a part of your daily life.

As you read on, you'll find a few tips and techniques on getting back to good, as well as words of encouragement and some profoundly inspirational quotes from many 'geniuses of generosity' on the following pages. Chapter 1 begins your journey in earnest with a 7 day campaign—start getting back to good today…and thank you so much!

Contents

tidbits
from the author

Ken...
Ken, wake up.
Ken, wake up, it's time...
KEN!

Ah, the dreaded wake up call. I have received many of these in my life. Sometimes my name is spoken softly, and other times shouted with a piercing scream. Often, these are literal wake up calls (usually from my wife and kids, or my buddy Kurt throwing rocks at my window trying to wake me up so I won't be late for work). But more often than not, they seem to be more metaphorical in nature. They trigger blinders to fall away and force me to look in new directions with fresh eyes and perspectives, completely transforming my perceptions and actions. If I'm truly listening, mindful, and aware, I can sometimes just make out a glimpse of a path I should be traveling.

With the hectic pace of the world today, and the negativity constantly bombarding us, we can become oblivious to any and all of the good we are given. When that happens, it is easy to forget or ignore our responsibility to share goodness and live with a grateful heart. Every so often though, we may get a little nudge or even a powerful shove from someone or something reminding us what is truly important in our lives.

These wake-up calls can open our eyes and encourage us to be more aware and attentive to what we are receiving and what we should be doing.

Also, they are great for reminding us to *not* take life for granted. Whether or not we pick up the phone and answer these calls…well, that's up to us. Just remember, if we don't answer now, we may have to answer for them later.

Wake up calls can be extraordinary things. Being a telephone repairman myself, perhaps you think I'm referring to those phone calls you get in a hotel. While that would be a very interesting topic for me to discuss (☎ just ask my family or close friends ☺), what I'm writing about here are those moments that gently sway you to think or act a little differently than you normally would, as well as those circumstances in life that literally shake you down to your core. Wake up calls can be so subtle you almost miss 'em; so perfect you'd swear someone is looking out for you, or so loud and devastating that you would like to turn in your get-out-of-jail-free card or request a do-over.

Have you ever been gently nudged into making changes in your life? Maybe it wasn't gentle at all—more like an unexpected punch in the stomach that knocks the wind out of you. Perhaps you've resisted change or didn't feel such encouragement was warranted. Nonetheless, I'll bet you have, at one time or another, felt guided to look closely at your life and draw up a new plan of action by changing the direction you were heading. Maybe zig instead of zag; take the next exit off the interstate rather than staying on your pre-planned route and completely change the course of your life…your relationships…your perspectives…your world.

Are you in the middle of one of those nudges now? Remember, these prods often appear when you least expect them. Something in your life may not be quite where you want it to be and for whatever reason, making goodness a priority may be timely for you (more than you may realize). If you can change one thought or perception for the better, make one apology, become more generous, give a moment of your time, clear your conscience and live with more health, selflessness and balance, it will all be worth it.

One small but vitally important reminder: do not let encounters with tragedies become your wake-up calls. Change your thoughts and actions now—do not wait until it becomes too late. Make amends for any wrongs you have caused, and live with goodness, not because you are forced to, but because it's the right thing to do.

Do you think we are getting wake-up calls to change? Calls for ourselves, our families, and our youth? Are we getting calls for society, humanity, and our planet? If you think we are, consider answering with a campaign for goodness. Not necessarily huge, not necessarily dramatic, just everyday people doing everyday things with a touch of goodness.

Do you hear the phone ringing? Maybe that's your wake-up call... go ahead, answer the phone, I'll wait. Remember, we never know what tomorrow will bring.

Live now, believe me,
wait not til tomorrow,
gather the roses of life today.

−*Pierre de Ronsard*

Before we go any further, my staff of advisors (okay, you got me, my lovely wife and kids) said at this point I should introduce myself. They said people would want to know a little about me and where I'm coming from, so I humbly offer my hand and say, "Hi, nice to meet you."

First, please allow me to share what I hope to inspire and accomplish with this campaign. I'm a firm believer in the fact that our world needs more goodness. Each and every one of us could be kinder, more giving, and generous—to ourselves, our families, those we come across everyday, as well as to our environment. Although it may be cliché, bringing more goodness into our world starts with that person staring back at you in the mirror.

When you share goodness, such as volunteering your time, helping a friend, donating, practicing your faith, rescuing an animal, or anything else that is genuinely good, do you ever get goose bumps or feel a chill go up your spine because you just inherently feel good about what you're doing? It's almost as if this is part of something greater, something we are supposed to do.

I completely trust and believe that we feel this way because doing good is a part of a much bigger picture—a picture that paints living with goodness as a *very* important, if not primary purpose for life. When you look close enough, this picture also subtly inspires us to share the love and compassion that exemplify the human spirit at its very highest and best.

Participating in the goodness campaign can help you improve your health, encourage better outlooks, and bring a more positive attitude to your life. You will see this bigger picture more clearly as well as the endless possibilities that come from consciously noticing your blessings, living with gratitude, and taking care of yourself. When you purposefully strive to live with more goodness, more of it finds you—trust me…something about goodness is divine.

I came across this tale many years ago, and just love the profound insight it crams into two little paragraphs, summing up the essence of the goodness campaign beautifully:

Native American Wisdom:
A Tale of Two Wolves

One evening, an old Cherokee told his grandson about a battle that goes on inside people. He said, "My son, the battle is between two wolves inside us all. The first wolf is evil. It is anger, envy, jealousy, sorrow, regret, greed, arrogance, self-pity, guilt, resentment, inferiority, lies, false pride, superiority, and ego.

The second wolf is good. It is joy, peace, love, hope, serenity, humility, kindness, benevolence, empathy, generosity, truth, compassion, and faith." The grandson thought about it for a moment and then asked his grandfather, "Which wolf wins?" The old Cherokee simply replied, "The one you feed."

—Author Unknown

I love this tale because of the powerful message it reveals in such a subtle and unassuming way. In every moment, we have a choice to notice the blessings we are given, say thank you, and focus positively. Or, in that same moment, we can choose to focus on the negative, scary, and unknown. As the snippet of wisdom from the tale demonstrates, we can *choose* to feed the good wolf and bring more encouragement, love, health, and happiness into our lives and the world.

I would like to share an example from my life when I fed that bad wolf (which grows big and strong quite quickly by the way), but then made a conscious decision to focus on feeding the good wolf instead—moving away from the negativity brought by fear, worry, stress, and anger; and encouraging more positive, peaceful, and promising thoughts and actions. I'm sure you can relate the tale to your life. How does it apply to you?

My boss just came out to visit me at the job site…he didn't like something I was doing…I sure hope I have this job tomorrow. Layoffs are all around, and work is so stressful. A great friend of mine called and said his cancer returned…I feel mad, sad, and worried for him and his family, but that pales in comparison to what he is going through. Hey! That guy just cut in front of me! My blood pressure rises while I fight a powerful urge to give him a gesture in the driver's seat.

Finances are getting worse; will I be able to care for my family? I am in a fight with my dad over something petty and stupid, but we're both too stubborn to make it right. On top of that, I'm out of shape and not living as healthy as I should. The kids have health issues…I worry so much about them.

As I watch the news, violence, greed, uncertainty, and selfishness really jump out at me. Where are we headed? What's the world going to be like for our children? I see a TV commercial showing some poor people suffering in poverty…my heart sinks in despair…how are we going to make it? How can I help? What's next? Who's there? How will I…?

Whoa! Whoa! Whoa! These thoughts, laced with fear and uncertainty, send me anxiously into a downward spiral of negativity. Life can indeed be hard and scary, but the more I think in this manner, the more anxious and stressed I become—a vicious and debilitating cycle. In this state of mind, remembering all the blessings and positives in my life are not exactly at the forefront of my thoughts; so I force myself to take a breath, and *stop this negative thinking* by consciously focusing on all that I have—on all I have been given. As soon as I take control and begin feeding the good wolf, a comforting path appears; quietly and humbly leading me to find solace and peace in that which is good and reassuring.

I say a prayer of thanks for what I have, and remember; no, scratch that—truly realize what I've been blessed with in my life. Then my mind begins to wander and I start thinking about my beloved grandma. She always had the knack of calming me and putting things into a positive light. She was from the old school, and spoke her mind openly and honestly. If something needed to be said, she had no reservations in doing so, often to the chagrin of the recipient (personal experience speaking here☺).

I'm smiling now as I write this and recollect her fortitude and insight. She was so wise, as are many of our elders. Life inevitably etches the knowledge of experience into a person over the years, and we should pull up a chair and an attentive, listening ear whenever possible, in order to gain knowledge and perspective from those who have walked the road before us…we could learn so much.

I digress. Getting back to my grandma, we called her Busia (boo-sha); she used to say, "Our world is going down the tubes." Often sitting in her favorite blue chair and crocheting away, she would offer her insights and say with a thick accent, "We (society in general) are heading in a bad direction. People are just not as grateful for what they have as they should be and feel entitled. They want too much, too quickly, and don't learn value. There is no patience or much concern for one another, and nothing good comes of this. Love is lost between family members, neighbors, and friends. People passing each other on the street lack common courtesy and kindness, and many people get sour and angry—just look how people drive. Things are not like they used to be."

I would sit on her bed and drink in her stories of yesteryear, about working as a baker in downtown Chicago circa the late the 1930's, making enormous pies. Her eyes would light up as she mused over reminiscing about enjoying the way patrons would scarf down her creations. "I used to make pies that were four inches thick," she said. "Back in those days, we took care of each other, and the pies were just one small example of that. My boss, Jimmy, would actually come by and make sure I wasn't being stingy with the ingredients. Jimmy would say, 'Don't be stingy with those ingredients! Don't be stingy.'"

She would speak ever softer, with a smile and far off look in her eyes—reliving the old days. "Now," as she brought her thoughts back to the present time and said frowning with a disapproving tone, "hmph, now life is a different story. Things are not like they were when I was young. People were nicer, kinder, and more generous. Life seemed simpler and much more meaningful. We took time to enjoy one another and what life had to offer."

As she spoke one day (this was probably some twenty years ago), I sat in silent disagreement. I was young, naïve, and full of optimism, thinking the world and life were great. But, as the years went on, I would hear this same story time and again, usually after dinner, but never before her nightly ritual of watching Wheel of Fortune. Trust me; nothing could get between Busia and 'the wheel.' But in all seriousness, each time we talked, we discussed the seemingly growing lack of goodness in the world, and I would understand a little more about what she was saying.

I know my grandma waxed nostalgic at times, but she was definitely onto something. Don't get me wrong, I know the past harbors scores of ills and demons right alongside the goodness it nurtured; and every moment in the present day there are billions of actions of goodness and kindness occurring around the world, but I think there is a fundamental shift away from goodness—from being as good as we can be. Almost everyone I speak with agrees that more kindness, care, compassion, and selflessness could play a bigger part in every aspect of our lives. The bottom line is that there is plenty of room for more goodness and kindness out there. What do you think?

Out there? I pause and ponder. Wait a second, Ken! There is plenty of room for more right here (I am tapping my heart). There is always plenty of room for more goodness in my life; I have thousands of opportunities to make *my* difference every day.

Contemplating my grandma's words and wisdom, I've spent a lot of time seriously thinking about what I could do to make my difference and change for the better. With every thought and action, I have the power to bring what she talked about into reality; right now, today. From the way I talk to and treat my family, to realizing what I have been given, to living with a grateful heart. I can help others physically, financially, and by lending an ear or wiping a tear. I can give a person encouragement or the benefit of the doubt, exercise and eat healthier, become a better parent, practice more patience and generosity at work and in my personal life, and last but not least, bite my tongue while I avoid making well-known hand gestures when driving. And that, my friend is just the start…there is so much more that can be done.

Our lives can always benefit from more goodness…our world definitely needs more. This is exactly why I feel compelled to start this campaign in my life—with that guy staring back at me in the mirror. I can immerse myself in goodness and take stock of what I have received and find new ways to reach out and share. In fact, every one of us can start our own campaign today doing something good—for ourselves, someone else, our kids, our families, friends, and for our planet—even a simple, beautiful smile fosters positive change.

Changing small things in everyday actions will not instantly bring about world peace, end world hunger, resolve that argument with your sister, or help you lose fifty pounds overnight; but living with goodness is as necessary to our lives as air. *All* thoughts and behaviors that are good will make a positive difference.

Oh, I'm sorry, there I go gabbing away and have not properly introduced myself. Hi, my name is Ken Ferrara, a thirty-something, typical family guy living near Chicago. I'm married with three kids, and continually learning that in order to be a better person, I must constantly focus on the good things in life—not the finer things, but the good ones.

I have been asked repeatedly why I'm qualified to write this book. My answer is always the same, "I'm simply a person trying to live a better life." I'm no more or less qualified than anyone else. I don't claim to always practice what I've written here and have made many mistakes. Undoubtedly, I will make more; but, that doesn't mean I can't keep moving forward and try to do a little something to make each day a little better. Do I stick to my campaign everyday? Of course not, but I can find ways to improve and do better as long as I keep trying.

This whole endeavor started approximately fourteen years ago when I found it therapeutic to pour my thoughts and feelings on scratch paper as I was going through some tough times with my family. Those notes contained reminders of all the blessings in my life, how I wanted to change for the better, and what I needed to do in order to accomplish those goals. Eventually, the scribbled-on papers coalesced into this book.

Even though I wrote much of these words years ago, I am embarrassed to say that quite often, and sometimes quite easily, I forget just how much I have been given and how much more I should be giving. But, I've learned to give myself the benefit of the doubt because life is an ongoing work in progress where a person can always make things better. With that, let's embark on our collective goodness campaign…and get back to good

1

goodness starts with me
7 days to change my world

Go ahead; say it, "Goodness starts with me." Now take a moment and really let those words take root. Mohandas Gandhi once said something similar, but infinitely more eloquent and thought provoking than I could ever hope to…he said,

You must be the change you wish to see in the world.

That profound quote from Gandhi contains insight into finding health, purpose, and happiness, as well as creating more care, compassion, and goodness in your life and our world. While that is a lot to ask from a group of 21 words, they become truly powerful when authentically put into action. What's that? There aren't 21 words; only twelve up there… hmmm, maybe my dyslexia was kicking in again. No, not this time, but you're right, there are only 12, so what's the story?

The group of 21 words comes from me adding a little twist to Gandhi's amazing inspirational quote, *"I must be the change I need in my life to be the change I wish to see in the world."* When you do this genuinely, you will discover myriad benefits including better health, improved relationships, attitudes of gratitude, and a more positive outlook. This, in turn, brings more goodness to you—it's a pleasant and nurturing cycle. All it takes is a little action…you'll see.

I'm sure you already participate in your own goodness campaign, because you are undoubtedly good at heart—a kind, caring, compassionate, and loving person. However, as I've said before, we all have occasions when we are *less than good*, and it's in these moments where we can consciously and actively find ways to better ourselves and become happier and healthier. What are the areas in life you can improve? Find a quiet moment and…

- **Look around**
- **Look closely**
- **Look deep inside.**

When you find an area or aspect of life where something is missing or needs a touch up—take action to clear it up. By doing so you will become more patient and experience a deeper sense of love, faith, compassion, and gratitude, as well as view life in a more positive light.

Solitude is the furnace of transformation.
—Henry Nouwen

When you are alone with your thoughts, and willing to take an honest look at yourself, much can be learned. Solitude can be a time of reflection to remember what you are grateful for, what you have accomplished, how you have lived, and what you still wish to achieve, change, and improve. Finding time to assess your life can be difficult, which is very understandable in the hectic, busy lives we lead today. But it has never been more important or relevant for you to make some time. How about right now?

I completely understand that due to life's many demands, your moments may have to be in the shower, before you go to bed, or on your lunch-break; but no matter where or when, try to find a few minutes for yourself each day and truly listen to what your conscience is telling you. Then, list what you would like to start changing and transforming in your life.

What I would like to improve in my life:

Date: _____

_____

_____

_____

_____

_____

_____

_____

_____

_____

_____

_____

_____

_____

_____

_____

_____

_____

_____

_____

_____

_____

_____

_____

_____

_____

_____

_____

_____

_____

_____

Thank you for taking the time to do this, and if you haven't yet, try to find one thing you can work on…just one. Everyone and everything around you becomes better when you improve *your* life! You may not change instantly; but you can change by applying one thought or action of goodness at a time.

I know that problems facing you today can seem daunting and unapproachable, leaving you feeling helpless to create any sort of real, positive change. Sometimes day-to-day life seems so hard, demanding, and unfair, that you may have little time, ambition, or energy to get back to good. You may even ask, "Can I really bring about change and make a difference by doing a little good every day?"

Absolutely! And there are powerful reasons to do just that. I'm sure you've heard the phrase, "a journey of a thousand miles begins with the first step," well, that same wisdom applies when you consciously strive to do something good for yourself and others. You are creating subtle, yet powerful ripple effects of goodness that will encompass your life, go out into the world, and then come back to you in countless ways.

You may not change your life or the world as in POW…Bang… BOOM; but you can change it for the better subtly; one person, one thought, one action…one day at a time—starting with yourself. Sure, you may not succeed everyday, but remember this: the more goodness you put out there, the more kindness you foster, and the more health and peace you seek, the more will find you. You can't always see it or notice it, but trust that it is there.

The days of our lives for all of us are numbered. We know that. And yes, there are certainly times when we aren't able to muster as much strength and patience as we would like. It's called being human. But I have found that in the simple act of living with hope, and in the daily effort to have a positive impact in the world, the days I do have are made all the more meaningful and precious. And for that, I am grateful.

-Elizabeth Edwards

This campaign is an easy way for you to actively take part in becoming more positive, caring, compassionate, and happy on a daily basis. Some dramatic changes you will see and feel almost instantly, while other benefits may take a little longer to develop. Since you have already completed your one-day, let's continue on, to the next step: *The Seven-Day.*

Your 7-day Goodness Campaign

To begin, I want to make sure you don't feel pressured to complete your campaign in seven consecutive days. If you are able to do it in a week, fantastic; but if not, no worries—simply do what you can, when you can, and try to keep moving forward and stay positive in your focus.

Our first step is going to be defining goodness...in a most general fashion. Now admittedly, that can be a little tricky because it is a highly subjective topic and means many different things to people. No matter what you call it or how you perceive it, goodness literally has the power to change your life. For our purposes here, we will keep it simple by describing goodness in a pure, elemental way: *that which is beneficial.* Just as important: *open to many diverse interpretations*—not solely associated with a single spiritual, cultural, or personal view. It is not exclusive, overbearing, or narrowly focused; rather, it is inclusive and encourages people to readily offer kindness, nurture tolerance and health, and exhibit selflessness.

You can use the following *goodness ring* as a basic description, and please write in your own words and concepts to personalize it as a guide for your campaign.

7-Day Journal

The following journal can be a great help for keeping track of what you are accomplishing, feeling, and seeing on a daily basis. By consciously thinking and writing about the good things you are doing, you will become immersed in this experience. Make your entries fun and inspiring snippets of your day, and enjoy this…it's only seven days….go for it! The journal is similar to the page you filled in earlier for your one-day campaign, but has one more entry.

Here's a quick recap:
    The first entry will consist of something you do for others; family, friends, a person you just met, or someone halfway around the world. Also, you can include anything you have done to help nature as well. The world is at your fingertips; be genuine and from the heart, and the ideas will come! Write down what you are doing, and if you like, you can include how you are feeling before and after your actions.
    The second entry will be something good for you. You can eat a healthy meal, exercise, take some time for yourself, say a prayer of thanks, or work on a project or goal you may have been putting off…you decide! Remember, these actions can be small or large…they can be fun or something a little more on the serious side (i.e. apologizing or forgiving someone).
    The third and final entry has two parts. First, realize one blessing in your life and be genuinely thankful for it. Second, take a moment to notice something beautiful in the world. This can be anything that touches your heart. Maybe you'll see a child finding comfort and solace in his mother's arms. If you happen to look up at a cloud contrasting a beautiful azure sky, take a moment and reflect on that magnificence. Perhaps you'll find beauty and peace in your faith. Maybe you are noticing healthy changes in your body from taking better care of yourself. How about those moments when laughing with your family, are you taking time to savor them? Were you blessed with health today? There is so much around us to be thankful for and truly notice; what will you find?

    You may not have entries for each topic every day, but when you feel something applies, be sure to write it down. By doing so, you are effectively training your mind to view people, situations, and life with a positive, compassionate, and patient perspective.

And some questions for you to consider once again:
- Do I treat others with less kindness, patience, and tolerance than I could?
- Do I take care of myself, eating a healthy diet, exercising, lowering the amount of stress in my life, and finding quality time for those important to me?
- Do I only care for myself by exclusively dealing with my needs, desires, and beliefs, leaving others to fend for themselves?
- Am I as generous and giving as I should be? As I could be?
- What makes me truly happy?
- What can I do to make my life, someone else's life, or the world better?
- Can I forgive someone and take the first step to make things right?
- What am I taking for granted today?
- Am I truly thankful for all that is in my life?

Remember, plenty of opportunities to think and act with more goodness in every aspect of life are present every day. You can make good choices that will bring immense benefits to you and other lives you touch. One gentle reminder...sometimes we have to look a little more at ourselves and what we should be doing, and perhaps be less critical toward others to see the countless opportunities of goodness that are buzzing around us constantly. Start doing something good today, and continue reading during your 7-day for more information and inspiration.

–Good Luck... have a great campaign!

My 7-day Goodness Campaign - Day 1

Date: _____

(circle what applies)

Good For Others: Family / Friends / Nature / Others:

_____

_____

_____

_____

_____

_____

_____

Good for Myself: Mind / Body / Spirit / Financial / Other:

_____

_____

_____

_____

_____

_____

_____

Today, I am grateful for & noticed
this beauty in our world ...

_____

_____

_____

_____

_____

_____

_____

The Most and Greatest

The greatest joy . . . . Giving
The ugliest personality trait. . . . . .Selfishness
The most satisfying work . . . . Helping Others

The most destructive habit. . . . . Worry
The worst thing to be without. . . . . Hope
The greatest problem to overcome . . . . Fear
The greatest asset. . . . . Faith

The greatest loss. . . . . Loss of Self-Respect
The most prized possession. . . . . Integrity
The most worthless emotion . . . . Self-Pity
The most contagious spirit . . . . Enthusiasm

The world's most powerful computer . . . . .The Brain
The most crippling disease of failure. . . . . Excuses
The two most power-filled words. . . . . I Can!
The two most difficult words to say . . . . I'm sorry

The deadliest weapon . . . . The Tongue
The greatest *Shot in the Arm* . . . . .Encouragement
The most dangerous pariah . . . . A Gossip
The most helpful thing to do . . . . Forgive

The most powerful force in life. . . . . Love
The most beautiful attire . . . . A Smile
The most effective sleeping pill. . . . . Peace of Mind
The strongest channel of communication . . . . .Prayer

—Unknown

My 7-day Goodness Campaign - Day 2

Date: _____

(circle what applies)

Good For Others: Family / Friends / Nature / Others:

_____

_____

_____

_____

_____

_____

_____

Good for Myself: Mind / Body / Spirit / Financial / Other:

_____

_____

_____

_____

_____

_____

Today, I am grateful for & noticed
this beauty in our world...

_____

_____

_____

_____

_____

_____

_____

An elderly woman slowly gathers her bags at the end of the checkout line and places them into her two-wheel cart for the walk home. She says good-bye to the cashier and begins taking small steps toward the automatic door. When the door opens, she starts fumbling with her cart; it seems one of her wheels has jammed up with a pebble. The last time this happened, it took her an hour to drag the cart home.

A man walking into the store takes notice of her struggle. "Here, let me give you a hand with that," he says. In about a second, he loosens the wheel so she can pull the cart freely once again. "Oh, God Bless you!" the woman exclaims with overwhelming gratitude. He makes her day and adds a little extra goodness into his life and our world.

My 7-day Goodness Campaign - Day 3

Date: _____

(circle what applies)

Good For Others: Family / Friends / Nature / Others:

_____

_____

_____

_____

_____

_____

Good for Myself: Mind / Body / Spirit / Financial / Other:

_____

_____

_____

_____

_____

Today, I am grateful for & noticed
this beauty in our world ...

_____

_____

_____

_____

_____

You have to give before you get.
You must plant your seeds before you reap the harvest.
The more you sow, the more you'll reap.
In giving to others, you'll find yourself truly blessed.
The law works to give you back more than you have sown.
The giver's harvest is always full.
Those who obtain have little. Those who scatter have much.
Nature does not give to those who will not spend.
-*Unknown*

My 7-day Goodness Campaign - Day 4

Date: _____

(circle what applies)

Good For Others: Family / Friends / Nature / Others:

_____

_____

_____

_____

_____

_____

Good for Myself: Mind / Body / Spirit / Financial / Other:

_____

_____

_____

_____

_____

_____

_____

Today, I am grateful for & noticed
this beauty in our world...

_____

_____

_____

_____

_____

_____

What can I do to improve my physical health?

You can do something right now! Make today the moment in time that you start living a healthier, more robust life. Start small…the changes will be amazing.

Perhaps you can eat healthier, walk around the block, or quit smoking. Drink a little more water today or create a plan for routine physical activity.

- Try to walk an extra 10-30 minutes today.
- Eat more natural, healthy foods. They are perfectly designed to fill you with just the right amounts of energy and nutrients, allowing your body to work to its full potential.
- Be conscious of food choices, levels of exercise, and medical conditions by incorporating healthy habits into your daily life.
- Don't forget to exercise those muscles in your face and share that smile!

What I am going to do? Be sure to consult your physician before any physical activity.

- _____
- _____
- _____
- _____

My 7-day Goodness Campaign - Day 5

Date: _____

(circle what applies)

Good For Others: Family / Friends / Nature / Others:

_____

_____

_____

_____

_____

_____

_____

Good for Myself: Mind / Body / Spirit / Financial / Other:

_____

_____

_____

_____

_____

_____

Today, I am grateful for & noticed
this beauty in our world ...

_____

_____

_____

_____

_____

_____

_____

There comes a time in every life when a person looks at the legacy he or she has left behind and absolutely understands that titles earned, statuses achieved, and material possessions are, at the end of the day, unimportant.

When looking back, you will understand that what you have accomplished and earned is far less important than how you have lived and treated others.

Real purpose…real meaning, often turns out to be living with a grateful heart, embracing honesty, kindness, love, compassion, faith, and sharing generously—in essence, living with goodness.

-ken ferrara

My 7-day Goodness Campaign - Day 6

Date:_____

(circle what applies)

Good For Others: Family / Friends / Nature / Others:

_____

_____

_____

_____

_____

_____

_____

Good for Myself: Mind / Body / Spirit / Financial / Other:

_____

_____

_____

_____

_____

_____

_____

Today, I am grateful for & noticed
this beauty in our world ...

_____

_____

_____

_____

_____

_____

Maybe someday we'll figure all this out,
try to put an end to all our doubt,
try to find a way to make things better now.

Maybe someday we'll live our lives out loud,
we'll be better off somehow…someday.

Sometimes we don't really notice just how good it can get.
So maybe we should start all over…start all over again.

-Rob Thomas, Someday, Cradlesong

My 7-day Goodness Campaign - Day 7

Date: _____

(circle what applies)

Good For Others: Family / Friends / Nature / Others:

_____

_____

_____

_____

_____

_____

Good for Myself: Mind / Body / Spirit / Financial / Other:

_____

_____

_____

_____

_____

_____

Today, I am grateful for & noticed
this beauty in our world...

_____

_____

_____

_____

_____

_____

You are making a real difference!

Continue building your momentum of goodness by finding new ways to share, give, be thankful, practice giving, and nurture your health. Please share the goodness campaign with others and inspire a few people to make it a part of their lives.

Now I invite you to learn more about getting back to good; an easy, thought-provoking process that will encourage you to remember, re-learn, and perhaps re-invent ways to share and experience more goodness and happiness! At the end of the book, I have provided a 30-day journal for you to document more of your life-changing campaign. Enjoy!

2

~~we can do this~~
we must do this...
a campaign for goodness

Advertising campaigns, political campaigns, campaigns against poverty and disease. All types of campaigns bombard us every day. They fulfill a vital service and purpose—to get a message across…to get the word out… to inspire us to take action. I think the time may be right for a goodness campaign. What do you think?

Our world seems to be in perpetual crisis; from wars, famine, and declining economies; to ruthless dictators and horrific natural disasters. *We hear it on the news*—theft, senseless violence, greed, selfishness, and unimaginable pain and suffering locally and around the globe. *We see it*—trouble in our own families, nature getting diminished and destroyed; angry, impatient people, personal and corporate greed, and a seemingly uncontrolled materialism that chokes and clouds our selfless instincts. *We feel it*—sickness and poor health, troubled relationships, stress from work, family, and personal issues, and the challenging uncertainty of the future.

While humanity is becoming more connected and technologically advanced every day, with more 'power' at our disposal than ever before, the world should be a nicer place. From the standpoint of our technologies and achievements, the world should be a more abundant, safe, and caring place to live, because we have the means and abilities to care for one another like no other moment in our history.

While our advancements are empowering, it is plain to see that humanity still has troubles. We often epitomize the very definition of goodness by loving, caring, giving selflessly, and showing compassion and tolerance toward one another, but the unfortunate reality is that in many ways, the opposite is also true. We can have problems with selfishness, negativity, and keeping positive perspectives.

On a personal level, you may not treat others as you should or perhaps feel hopeless and negative from time to time; let's face it, the demands and uncertainties of life can easily cause a person to become anxious and stressed. At other times, you may feel life lacks meaning, purpose, or direction. On a larger scale, countries wage war, there is immense, crushing poverty and famine around the world, and people continue trying to justify differences, rather than focusing on and embracing our common ties.

I often wonder why people are selfish (myself *always* included). Why are we rude and indifferent, often simply caring for our own? Why do we not see the absolute bounty and beauty in front of us every day? What prompts a person to live a life of excess while so many others scrounge for food, health, and shelter every day? Why does one person believe his or her children, possessions, beliefs, or rights are more important than yours? Or vice versa?

Which of the following is a better description of the world to you?

hate wAR
selfishness
GREED wrong Violence
disaster
Negative ANGER dread
homeless
Gangs hopeless indifference
evil
poverty
stress rude
poor anxiety disease
FAMINE
RACISM
road rage loss
Inconsiderate
uncertainty

Or...the goodness ring.

The words of negativity can describe our world quite often; perhaps even more than the ones in the goodness ring…not all the time, but certainly quite often. Maybe it's because bad news sells more, or the proliferation of the Internet allows us unfettered access to all of this negative stuff; but in my opinion, there is plenty of negativity out there, and that is frightening. The things those words describe are real. Evil exists and rears its ugly head day after day without rest; violence and bloodshed, arguments, fights, death and disheartenment occur every day. These things are very scary and unsettling. Of that, there is no question.

On the bright side though, we have the power to change what those negative words describe and collectively bring more goodness into our world. You have the ability to bring more of it into your life right now, today…and the next day…and the next day…and the next. For as much as I am heart-broken, disappointed, and scared by the evil and wrongdoing in our world; for as much as I stress and worry about what tomorrow will bring my loved ones, humanity, and our world, I constantly marvel at the power of goodness—it is wonderfully inspiring.

Ask people you know if they feel the world needs more goodness. Now, ask yourself that very same question. I'm willing to bet the answer is probably a resounding *yes!* We could be kinder, healthier, more caring, compassionate, and giving; but how can these things become a bigger part of our lives? One powerfully inspiring answer starts with that person staring back at you in the mirror. Creating well-being in your life by making small adjustments in your actions and attitudes, and taking a few moments to care for others enables you to become a powerful creator of goodness.

People are inherently good. Because of that fact, there is a responsibility for living with goodness that applies to everyone; from the poor to the rich; from heads of state to followers and leaders of differing spiritual beliefs; from business and community leaders to famous, powerful, and everyday people. Creed, culture, country, and social class, as well as variations in ideology, upbringing, and personality make no difference—everyone is responsible to live with goodness.

In the biggest possible picture, there is no "us against them," or "you against me," as we are all in this together. Of course, we must provide and care for ourselves, protect what we hold dear and will feel connected to our individual beliefs, feelings, and actions; but in the end, one of the most crucial battles we'll face is to live with goodness to the best of our abilities—we are accountable for that.

But we can perhaps remember, if only for a time, that those who live with us are our brothers, that they share with us the same short moment of life; that they seek, as do we, nothing but the chance to live out their lives in purpose and in happiness, winning what satisfaction and fulfillment they can.
-Robert F. Kennedy

On the surface, our lives may seem to have little in common. A young couple raising three kids in Nebraska may feel worlds away from an orphaned child growing up half-way around the world…they are connected. A homeless man may not feel any commonality to a prominent business leader or politician…but they share a common bond. A newborn baby girl held by her ninety-five year old great grandmother…linked beyond family ties.

Whatever community or country we are a part of; regardless of personal lifestyles, beliefs, or opinions, each of us can do our part to collectively strengthen the human spirit of goodness. Simple thoughts and actions can bring our world back to good billions of times a day, and the potential is exponential when each of us takes part in the effort. Peace, compromise, prosperity, fulfillment, and happiness are the potential harvest when we find and travel unique paths to the common goal of true goodness. The choice is each of ours alone. Let's do our best to bring more of it into our world each day to make life better for our children and beyond.

imagine the possibilities…

☑ <u>My Goodness Campaign</u>

❑ Love and serve kindly—to the best of my ability.

❑ Offer the benefit of the doubt.

❑ Have Faith.

❑ Live a healthy lifestyle.

❑ Live with a grateful Heart.

❑ Treat others as I would like to be treated.

3

getting back to good

All people have a basic decency and goodness. If they listen to it and act on it, they are giving a great deal of what it is the world needs most. It is not complicated, but it takes courage. It takes courage for people to listen to their own good.

—Pablo Casals

Getting back to good. That may be a somewhat curious phrase, but what exactly does it mean? Well, to put it simply, a set of straightforward ideas, principles, and actions that inspire, remind, and invite you to identify and apply positive attitudes and actions in everyday life. These ideas have been around for ages, and when they are consistently applied, even on a small scale, they effectively eliminate negativity and enhance positivity and goodness. Most importantly, they are customizable to fit your life by the person who knows that life best—you!

As I said before, the word goodness means many different things to people. For some, goodness is God, to others it is the inherent desire to help fellow human beings, care for nature, and ourselves. It can represent healing the sick and feeding the hungry and encompasses every aspect of life. No matter what you call it or how you perceive it, the all-encompassing power of goodness changes perspectives and improves lives—starting with your own. You quite literally have the power to change the world.

For centuries, philosophers, theologians, and scholars have debated issues surrounding the true nature of goodness, but it is not as complex as we make it out to seem. Various cultures and individuals have diverse ideas and beliefs, inevitably leading to differing perspectives. While these different outlooks and views have inspired the closeness, co-operation, compassion, and care of the human spirit, they have also spawned separation, prejudice, intolerance, and hatred (ironically, often committed in the name of goodness) Regardless of any negativity experienced in the past, we will make a commitment to keep moving forward.

Our inherent knowledge of goodness, whether that's expressed by being kind and compassionate with others, feeling awe-struck when looking up at the stars and standing next to the ocean, or surrounding and immersing ourselves in that which is good and healthy, can only be applied by choice and effort. Much like a muscle, this knowledge must be used often in order to keep it functional and strong. When a muscle is not used, it becomes weak, frail, susceptible to damage, and unable to function properly. Similarly, when we do not choose to apply our inherent sense of goodness, it becomes weak and unable to function as designed, giving way to negativity, selfishness, and unhealthy attitudes and outlooks.

Speaking of being positive, imagine a table in front of you. On that table sits a glass filled exactly halfway to the top with water. Now, if you ask different people to describe what they see, you are likely to get many different answers, but they likely can be separated into four descriptions. *The first*, which is optimistic, positive, and cheerful, is that the glass is half-full (for some people, that equates to overflowing). With this perspective, the glass has plenty of water; you can enjoy it, share it with others, and feel good about it. *The second* is a little on the pessimistic side—stating that the glass is half-empty. When this is your perspective, you worry if there will be enough water for yourself, so you don't share as much as you should and constantly think about having enough. *The third* description is that there simply is a glass there and 'it is what it is.' The fourth and final view is the most negative of the bunch, "What glass are you talking about? I don't see a glass."

What does that glass of water look like to you? On the full side? On the empty side? Simply a glass of water on a table? Or, "What glass?" As life brings us our personal blessings and trials, each of us can describe our own glass of water in every one of those ways; I know I certainly have. Take a moment and think about the glass that represents your life. How does it look to you? What could you do to make it overflow?

I was talking with my teen-aged daughter about the 'glass half-full concept' one day. She rolled her eyes and said "Dad, give me a break. There is no such thing as a glass half-full or half-empty, there's only a glass with water in it—I'm a realist." To that I replied, "You may be Gina, but the way you look at that glass can make all the difference. It's all about perspective. If you don't see the glass as half-full or half-empty, how about looking at it like this…" and I gave her this:

A pessimist, they say, sees a glass of water as being half empty; an optimist sees the same glass as half full. But a giving person sees a glass of water and starts looking for someone who might be thirsty.

-G. Donald Gale

After she read it over and again, her expression softened and I said, "Maybe you are a realist…but no matter how you perceive or what you believe, never forget to be a giving person." She then walked away mumbling something about "…Whatever, Dad," but I can see she got the message through her actions, and I'm proud of her.

Is it possible for someone to be positive all the time? Of course not, we are all human, and have moments we may be less than proud of; let's face it, we'll have more. Having said that, I want to firmly impress upon you that we—you and me and everyone we know—have the power to make a positive difference in our own lives as well as in the lives around us.

Despite the cliché, living with goodness becomes its own, fantastic reward, on a personal level as well as on a grand scale. Actively seeking to become a better person for yourself and others around you will move you toward a more positive and enriching life that will encourage you to:
- Find more happiness and a peaceful sense of fulfillment;
- Deal with situations and your relationships more positively, with abundant patience; Constantly remember what you should be thankful for, from your health to your family and friends to nature, even the day itself;
- Show tolerance of the dynamic diversity in our world, from the multitude of differing spiritual beliefs to widely varying personal views and appearances;
- Care for yourself physically, emotionally, and spiritually;
- Mend broken or faltering relationships;
- Demonstrate kindness and gratitude, even through the challenging circumstances life inevitably brings;

- Offer apologies and forgiveness to those you have hurt, as well as to those who've hurt you;
- Find meaning and purpose for life by learning to live for more than yourself;
- Realize peace of mind.

These points will become reality for you when you choose to think positively and take ACTion. One easy way for you to take action is to participate in your own goodness campaign. I know you believe in your ability to make a difference because you've read this far. I'm really excited, because your positive potential is limitless.

Following are some general guidelines, if you will, for getting back to good. I want to emphasize that these are in no particular order, and will have varying degrees of significance for you, because what is important to you can only be decided by, that's right—you.

getting back to good

- Have faith. (This is, of course, different and unique for everyone, but can include having faith spiritually, in yourself, and in the goodness of humanity.)
- Live with a grateful heart for all that comes into your life, both good and (seemingly) bad. Give thanks in thought, word, and action.
- Look within to change selfishness into selflessness.
- Nurture all aspects of health. You must feel good about yourself in order to help others to the best of your ability.
- Practice giving. Give help, patience, tolerance, and kindness; give forgiveness, love, and care for others. Give as much as possible; nothing is too big or small.
- Simply be good…and nice. Continually foster as much goodness as possible. There will be times when you may falter, but always work to find your way back to good.

- Be tolerant and respectful of the dynamic diversity in our world, from the multitude of differing spiritual beliefs to widely varying personal views and appearances.
- Demonstrate kindness and gratitude, even through the challenging circumstances life inevitably brings.
- Offer apologies and forgiveness to those you have hurt, as well as to those who've hurt you.

Will you be able to fix problems in your life by getting back to good? Absolutely! Many troubles, problems, and day-to-day inconveniences can be thoroughly resolved if you make an honest effort to live with more goodness. You may find challenges facing you are actually caused by, ready for this—you…by your thoughts and actions.

For example:
- Do I treat people as I want to be treated?
- How do I deal with adversity?
- Do I take care of myself as I should?
- Is my faith strong?
- Am I a persistent optimist, or constant pessimist?
- Do I wallow in self-pity when life doesn't go my way, or do I accentuate the positives?

When life gets tough, as it certainly can, tend to your challenges by doing what is necessary to fix them, but do so with the care, compassion, and positive attitudes emphasized by getting back to good. Your perspective can change from one of *What about me?* or *Why me?* or *My way is the only way;* to one of overwhelming selflessness and care for others. Also, negative people and situations will no longer affect you the same way.

Remember, getting back to good is not an immediate solution for the troubles and problems of your life or for the problems of our world; but simply because it may not be immediate does not mean it isn't worthwhile. Becoming the change you need in your life in order to live with more goodness is one of the best things you can do with your precious time here.

Ask yourself: Who am I? Who do I want to be? How can I make my difference? What am I meant to do with my life? Another big question is, "Am I truly happy and fulfilled?" Not in the sense that you have visited those places you've dreamt about, climbed the corporate ladder, or achieved material goals. No, what I'm talking about is the fulfillment that comes from knowing you have done your best to be the change you want to see in your life and in our world. To know you have fulfilled your purpose here so completely with respect to caring for yourself and others, that if you lay your head down for the last time tonight, you could truly rest and find peace. Having said that, would you be ready, confident, and secure in knowing you have done your best? Or, will you have regrets when your time comes?

All of this goodness stuff sounds good in theory, I know; but in order for it to make a real difference, well, that depends on what you decide to do. You see, the ways you decide to think and act every day will be the drivers and catalysts for change. How successful can you be? The sky's the limit, and that limit is set by you!

No matter what is written in a book, how much sense it makes, or how good it sounds, you are ultimately in control of how effective it will be. And while it may be easy to go through a list of people in your mind who you think need to get back to good more than you, please try your best to keep the focus on yourself (*wink wink* I have trouble with that one).

*It is not what they profess, but what
they practice that makes them good.*

–Greek Proverb

Getting back to good is not as simple as saying, "Practice what you preach," or, "Just be good." As human beings, we are very complex and easily affected by different situations and circumstances that constantly shape and mold our choices and actions. Just as the Greek proverb states, we can profess all we want, but where the rubber meets the road is what really counts.

Goodness can be easily complicated with details, complex guidelines, and principles, but ultimately it is pure and pretty simple—but that's not to say it's necessarily easy. It's kind of like losing weight. We all know what we should be doing—eating healthy and exercising—simple, right. Ah, but the follow through, that's where it can get a tad difficult. But just because something may prove to be challenging doesn't mean we should shy away from it. No, just the opposite…head right for it and step right in, whether getting healthy or encouraging your inherent knowledge of goodness… choose to follow through with positive thoughts and actions in ways that are right for you.

Share with people you know and learn from them at the same time. Try to engage family, friends, acquaintances, and those you don't know with compromise and compassion, while not segregating or alienating the many different ways other people choose to express their views. Differing perspectives and characteristics can be beautiful and eye-opening, so remember to *include* rather than exclude different people, ideas, and beliefs.

Always recognize the power you have to take charge of situations and circumstances in your life. Become aware of what and where you can improve, and start thinking about how you can make a difference—in your life, and just as importantly, in the lives of others. Remember the wisdom from the old Cherokee, "Which wolf wins? The one you feed." By feeding your *good wolf,* you can effectively bring about immensely powerful, beneficial, and positive changes to your life.

There is always room for improvement—always a chance to get back to good in some way. You can forgive, and at the same time, apologize and seek forgiveness from others. Health, in all of its facets and forms, needs to be constantly developed and enhanced. Physical well-being is one important aspect, but you can always work on improving spiritual and emotional health, too. I know you thought about this already, but think about it again, what can you improve? Take a moment, grab a piece of paper and a pen, or use the 'my goodness campaign goals' page here, and continue your list of things you would like to improve in your life.

Setting Goals:

Goal setting is a powerful process for thinking about what you want to accomplish and motivates you to turn your vision of the future into reality. The process of setting goals helps you achieve what you desire, and guides you to concentrate your energies to get it.

Goals can be incredibly motivating; take a moment and set some goals for yourself. Write down why you want to accomplish these goals and when you intend on completing them. You may want to get back to good health by committing to change your lifestyle. Perhaps you will set a goal of being thankful every day and reflect on your blessings in a gratitude journal. Maybe you will take the first step to fix a relationship with someone close to you. These positive intentions will bring new and powerful direction and focus to your life.

Get back to good and continue your personal campaign, whether that's as a parent, a caring person, a student, a family member, or a friend; as a teacher, a religious/spiritual leader and follower, an employee, the head of a company, or the head of a nation.

My Goodness Campaign Goals:
Date:_____

- _____
- _____
- _____
- _____
- _____
- _____
- _____
- _____
- _____
- _____
- _____
- _____

4

having faith

*Take the first step in faith. You don't have to
see the whole staircase, just take the first step.*

–Dr. Martin Luther King, Jr.

Faith gives stability and purpose to life, and has a personal, unique meaning for everyone. Generally, it can be described as trust, confidence, devotion, conviction, belief, and loyalty, as well as much more. We each have a degree of faith in our abilities and ourselves, but in the context of goodness, it often means a connection to something greater. That connection can be expressed in a multitude of ways. While it is certainly linked to religion and spirituality for many people, for others it is expressed in more personal forms.

You have the prerogative to define and interpret what faith means to you. Having faith in something more than the here and now, in the goodness of humankind, nature, science, and yourself are a few ways you can define it; you can even choose to have faith in randomness and happenstance—the choice is yours. Regardless of what you believe, whether secular, spiritual, or personal, rest assured that faith remains a common thread tying humanity together. It binds you to me, and both of us to every person on the planet.

Unfortunately, much time and energy is spent on negatively pointing out differences of the various creeds, beliefs, and convictions of humanity. Since I started writing the many manifestations of this book, some similar questions have popped up repeatedly. The questions come in many forms, with differing intentions; but they often center on spiritual beliefs, religions, or belief systems.

After several chapters were written and rewritten, added, removed, and mulled over, I would like to share my personal opinion on the subject: What I think about faith, regarding religions, belief systems, and spiritual or personal views means nothing for you—the only important things are what you choose to have faith in and believe. The only suggestions this book has regarding faith are that you to try your best to make a constant effort for goodness to be present in your everyday life and to be tolerant.

Every person has a unique opinion and outlook regarding faith, some spiritual and some not (even having no belief is a unique spiritual view); regardless, I believe we are born with an innate knowledge of goodness. Many people believe this innate knowledge comes from God or a higher power. To others, goodness is a trait that is hard-wired into the human psyche. I respectfully leave the debates and intricacies surrounding various faiths and belief systems to those more learned than myself, and instead wish to focus on one very important purpose of our lives that is the cornerstone of all true faiths...living with goodness.

Faith should not cause or encourage intolerance, indifference, or violence, even to the smallest degree. That being said, no one can deny the innate calling of spirituality throughout humanity, as the various, beautiful religions and belief systems of the world so vividly convey. All connections to goodness, whether personal or of an organized nature, commonly share basic tenets—to think and live with goodness and humility, to be thankful, selfless, kind, and tolerant (essentially the foundation for the Ethic of Reciprocity or Golden-Rule). Of course, specific views, beliefs, practices, sacred doctrines and texts differentiate various belief systems, but they can all help, each in their own, unique way, to guide us live with more goodness.

focus on goodness, love, and tolerance

You are the only one who knows what works and feels right for yourself, therefore, your view of faith will always be something that is truth for you. No matter what your perspectives are, the responsibility to live with goodness crosses all boundaries, separations, religions, and views. Let's give each other room to believe, worship, and rationalize in our own, unique ways, and constantly focus on living with and sharing more goodness.

Ideally, diverse views should be respected, but that is simply not the case much of the time. Spiritual convictions are often so strong and profound that respecting different views can be difficult, leading to the ubiquitous problem of intolerance. When people try to force their convictions onto others, complications inevitably result. This often sours faith with intolerance and separation, leading away from the very goodness that teaches us to become as tolerant as possible in every aspect of life.

Religions are many and diverse,
but reason and goodness are one.

–Elbert Hubbard

Learn to look beyond personal prejudice or bias toward different beliefs and creeds by acknowledging the goodness all faiths and beliefs can share. Ultimately, you will choose a connection to goodness that feels right and works for you. Please give others the freedom to do the same. Remember, goodness is a tie that binds, and spiritual interpretations that are laced with intolerance break that binding tie.

Even though much of humanity maintains spiritual beliefs, and countless houses of worship instruct followers to live with goodness, the unfortunate reality is that many of those teachings do not make it out the front door to become thoughts and actions in the world. Similarly, inspired instructions of goodness from many holy texts, read by billions of people of various beliefs, do not make it off the written page to become thoughts and actions as often as they could. Instead, spiritual beliefs can become selfishly incorporated into personal needs, wants, and desires.

Your choice to have faith is free and personal, and the manner in which you make that connection is unique and individual. But let us always remember and hold this fact close to our hearts—choosing to have faith means having the responsibility to think and act with goodness to the best of our ability.

5

look up...
living with a grateful heart

Gratitude is not only the greatest
of virtues, but the parent of all the others.

–Marcus Tullius Cicero

As I walk out my apartment each morning, I look at the plaque hung purposefully next to the door; it reads, *Begin Each Day with a Grateful Heart*. Truly living by those words puts every day into a positive light. Saying thank you for what we receive in life is one of the greatest things we can do. We can offer thanks to others for holding a door open, for helping us through tough situations, and for giving us gifts. A thankful perspective is so powerful that you can find happiness and peace of mind, no matter what challenges come your way.

We may forget to say thank you or not feel grateful for what we receive every day, and that can lead to feelings of entitlement and negativity. Without a thankful perspective, you can become unhappy or despondent even when life is going well and you have a great state of affairs. I am the first to admit it... feeling grateful when all is going well is pretty easy; after all, when everything is going your way, it can be tough to find things to complain about. However, losing an outlook of gratitude can be equally as easy when challenging situations or tough times become a part of life.

Ideally, gratitude should be practiced daily. This is not always possible, but in this chapter, you'll find ways to perceive life in a more positive, grateful way. Remember, while being genuinely thankful is very important, it is only part of the equation of gratitude; acting thankfully completes it.

> *As we express our gratitude, we must*
> *never forget that the highest appreciation*
> *is not to utter words, but to live by them.*

> *–John F Kennedy*

Foundations of Thankfulness

In order to achieve and maintain an attitude of gratitude, it is necessary to strengthen views and actions that support your foundation of thankfulness and remove obstacles that chip and rot that foundation away. No one can force you to feel grateful or see the goodness and positive things in your life; that must come from you.

- **Remember and strengthen these views:**
    Be grateful for...
    - each new day
    - health
    - abilities

- **Remove obstacles:**
    - taking for granted/feeling entitled
    - dealing with tough, tragic times without a thankful perspective
    - self-pity
    - worrying about what is out of your control

- **Maintain your thankful perspective:**
    - your thankful checklist/gratitude journal
    - that's life!
    - thankfulness can be achieved

simply be thankful

Although it may not be possible to feel genuinely grateful all the time, wholeheartedly trying to keep a strong attitude of gratitude can lead to a life without overwhelming problems, struggles, or hardship. This is not to say you won't experience tough, troubling, or challenging situations, because everyone does; but it can powerfully combat and counteract the negative effects of stress and adversity.

Try to be mindful of the fact that everything in life is given to you— even the day itself. Sure, you may own things on paper or have your name associated with achievements, titles, or positions, but ultimately you only have such things because they have been given. Make an effort to show gratitude every day with your thoughts *and* through your actions.

grateful for each new day

Feeling thankful for waking each day, and for what you have in your life is very important, but it is also vital to remember the collective gift we receive with every new sunrise. The possibility does exist, that life-altering circumstances, such as meteor impacts, super-volcanic eruptions, or other catastrophic disasters could befall our planet at any time and totally annihilate life as we know it. Granted, the odds of such events are small, but nonetheless the chance is real. There is always the more realistic prospect of the "smaller," natural disasters that could throw our lives into chaos at any time around the neighborhood or around the globe. These scenarios are not written to scare or intimidate, but rather to remind; to help us remember just how reliant we are on nature and the world that sustains us, and to be thankful for each day we receive.

Each day's a gift…not a given right

–Nickelback

We have invented, discovered, and created many magnificent things, but they pale in comparison to the natural world. Our technological advancements and discoveries are insignificant when contrasted by forces of nature. When we become overconfident in our abilities, we can easily forget that our 'power' is fragile and feeble. Any human progress and achievement relies on the fact that we are given each new day. To be totally honest, our technological advancements are not possible without the opportunities that nature, or if you are so inclined, a higher power / God afford us.

Life exists on this planet only as long as the sun continues to shine and rain continues to fall. Be grateful for each new day by acknowledging every day as a gift that should not be taken for granted. Be humble and show thanks for the awesome power and splendor of nature by treating it with respect.

thankful for health

Once you have offered thanks for the dawning of each new day, be thankful for the health you have. The first step in doing so is recognizing that health is ultimately out of your control. Of course, you have the responsibility to care for yourself, but even if you work diligently to maintain a healthy lifestyle, you can become afflicted with disease and disability. When blessed with health in any aspect, be thankful by using it to bring more goodness into your life.

Everything in nature is designed to have a limited existence, from the six-hundred-year-old redwood tree to the three-day life of a mosquito. Try not to feel mad, sad, or cheated when health problems confront you, as aging and illness are a natural part of life. When self-pity takes over, we can start asking, "Why? Why me? Why do I have to suffer?" In truth, the question we should be asking is, "Why not me?" Always remember to be thankful for health, because it can be gone in an instant!

thankful for ability

Recognizing natural abilities as gifts is one thing that can be forgotten quite easily. In order to achieve goals, you may have to sacrifice and toil through difficult situations by working diligently, giving you a deserved feeling of pride and satisfaction. Those feelings are normal and healthy, but always remember that while you must put forth the effort, sacrifice, and work for your achievements, the fundamental reasons you are able to accomplish them is because you are given what you need to do so (i.e. the day itself, health, talents, etc.).

An overabundance of pride in your abilities or achievements can lead to feelings of superiority, self-importance, and arrogance—not things that are in any way associated with a thankful perspective. Do you know people who treat others poorly simply because of differing degrees of material possessions, abilities, status, or achievements? If you recognize these behaviors in yourself, immediately take thankful action by grounding yourself to the fact that you are given what you need in order to achieve what you attain. Remember, we are all equal, no matter status or pursuits in life.

A thankful perspective, with regard to your achievements and abilities, means feeling blessed to be as smart, creative, and successful as you have been. When you view abilities as gifts, you will not feel superior; instead, you will treat others equally—with respect, no matter how accomplishments, status, educational levels, or social groups differ from your own.

Removing Obstacles

Reducing obstacles that hinder an attitude of gratitude is the next necessary step to a thankful perspective. Learn to recognize when and where these obstacles appear in your life, and work to remove them.

taking for granted

"Don't take life for granted." That phrase is very clichéd—only because it is so true. We can take many aspects of life for granted by forgetting or overlooking the fact that everything we have are gifts. Too often, life is turned upside down in the blink of an eye by hardship or tragedy, and unfortunately, this is often the only time many of us realize our blessings. Another cliché testifies to that fact: "You don't know what you've got until it's gone." The wisdom of these sayings is not to be ignored. You can agree with them now or be forced to accept them later.

In order to become more thankful, start with the simple act of noticing what you have in front of you every day. I know this can seem quite simplistic, but making a list of all you are grateful for, and establishing a daily routine to reflect on these gifts can greatly enhance your ability to notice what you have in your life. By being grateful for your health, your loved ones, and each new day, you will be *choosing* to take nothing for granted.

Do you ever find yourself feeling entitled? When you take life for granted, a sense of entitlement frequently follows. Believing you are owed a nice, healthy, prosperous, and rewarding life is different from being genuinely thankful for those things. Try to view health, happiness, and life itself from a grateful perspective rather than from one of entitlement. Take some time each day…just a couple of moments, and express gratitude for your blessings. Always try to remain thankful for the fact that you are given the ability to achieve and accomplish, and transform any sense of entitlement into actions of goodness.

coping with tough & tragic times

Terrifying stories or occurrences of hardship, injury, tragedy, and death have touched every one of us in some way. We hear about them on the news, from people we know, or firsthand through personal experiences. When tragedy strikes, it can be shocking and horrifying. Unfortunately, this is often the only time our eyes are truly open to the reality of what belongs to us—*nothing*. No amount of money or perceived power can undo a tragic accident or death, control nature, or stop undesirable things from happening; they are forever beyond our control.

During tough and tragic times, a selfish, thankless attitude causes you to feel slighted and treated unfairly. I have often heard people exclaim (as well as thought this way myself), "How could this to happen? Why is this happening to me? It's not fair!" When you think in such a manner, you are not living with gratitude. Remembering all you should be grateful for makes coping with challenges and troubles more effective, if not altogether easier. Here are a few helpful ideas…

…cope by trusting faithfully

Tough, tragic times can be very difficult to get through. During times of strife, emotions can run the gamut from despair to hope to helplessness. While emotions play a vital role in helping you cope with any pain, hurt, confusion, and anger you may be feeling, you can purposefully apply positive thoughts and actions to lessen the severity and duration of difficult situations.

For instance, if you don't understand why bad things happen, try placing trust in your faith with an attitude of gratitude—this can help replace pain with a healing perspective of understanding. How many times has something bad happened that was very difficult to deal with, but in the end turned out to be good? Another cliché comes to mind: "a blessing in disguise."

Why do bad things happen? Sometimes there are no answers to questions about why. Perhaps the reasons for dire life events or hardships will be learned later in life, or even after life. Above all, put faith and trust in goodness.

…accept that adversity is a fact of life

Adversity strikes everyone. Loved ones are lost; family members, friends, and innocent people experience tragedy every day. Debilitating illnesses grab hold of people, forcefully squeezing and choking the life out of them. Forces of nature create havoc, tragic accidents occur, and chasms created by humankind all serve to seize life, health, and happiness.

How can anyone effectively cope with such things? One way to deal with adversity is to accept it as a natural part of life—in that difficulty and hardship will not always find someone else or happen to "the other person." When adversity appears, try to find a way to effectively cope and understand what you need to learn from it. Although finding gratitude in some situations may seem impossible, confront adversity with the strength and positive attitude a thankful perspective provides.

...remember that almost every situation could be worse

Try not to be caught up in the "Why me?" syndrome, which combines discouragement with self-pity. When facing tough times or hardship, you may feel horrible, helpless, and angry; please try to stop. Even though these emotions and feelings are part of a natural coping process, try to be thankful your circumstances are only as bad as they are, remembering that almost every situation could be worse. When dealing with adversity, you may not be able to change your situation, but what you can change is your perspective and how you deal with your conditions.

One way to do this is to visualize completely unbearable circumstances. For example, if a loved one has suffered traumatic injuries in an accident, you will undoubtedly be scared, worried, and feel terrible about seeing her in such a position. However, imagine you lost your loved one in that accident. Think and reflect upon what that would be like. Dream in vivid detail about the memorial service, the lonely holidays, and the emptiness in your home; then jump back to reality and be thankful for what you do have—more than likely, your situation is not as bad as it could be.

Another method that works for bringing me out of a self-imposed pity-party is to add one item of loss to my current situation. For instance, when I was transferred to a new location at work, with a commute that was an hour longer, I was upset...very upset. However, in order to keep it in perspective, I added one item of loss to this situation: I imagined losing my job. When I really thought about losing my job in vivid detail, my current situation of only being transferred became much more manageable; I even felt grateful.

Now, let's take it a step further...say I just lost my job; I would be pretty distraught and upset. In order to change my perspective, I would add one item of loss to this situation. I would imagine losing my job while just being diagnosed with cancer one-week prior…makes losing the job a little easier to deal with. One final example, let's say I was just diagnosed with cancer, and lost my job, but then found out my teen-aged daughter was paralyzed (or worse) in an accident.

You see where I'm going with this…almost every situation could be worse. I know that trying to envision bad circumstances can be understandably difficult, but it is an exercise that encourages you to see that almost every situation could be worse. By doing so, it can help you keep a perspective of thankfulness for what you are really blessed with in your life.

Sometimes people face circumstances where they feel that they cannot imagine anything worse, such as the loss of a loved one. At this point, faith, family, and friends often become life-saving support. When enduring the loss of a loved one, remember to be grateful for what you had—the touch, the time, the smiles, and the love—do not forget those things. At the very least, feel thankful and blessed for the time you were given.

Think of one thing in your life right now that you are unhappy about…a situation…person…job…etc. and write down imaginary scenarios adding one item of loss to remind yourself that every situation could be worse:

Situation(s):

_____

_____

_____

_____

_____

_____

_____

_____

_____

How it could be worse:

_____

_____

_____

_____

_____

_____

_____

_____

_____

...remember times when you were blessed—or downright lucky!

When you are facing adversity, think about a day or situation you are grateful for when you were lucky or had the proverbial guardian angel on your shoulder (I'm sure you have at least one, and likely many more). Take some time to reflect on those *lucky days* in your life, write them down, and feel grateful. Use this feeling to change your perspective to an attitude of gratitude, and you will deal with adversity in a much more positive way.

Let me give you one example from my life. Back when I was living at home with my folks in the late nineties, I worked the afternoon shift at the phone company. My parents worked early in the morning and didn't get home until five, so every day I would let our dogs out in the yard before I left. This day started out like every other; I woke up, said good-by to my parents as they left for work, and went about my morning routine. I worked out, showered, wasted time in front of the TV and computer, and let the dogs out.

Around eleven, it was time to go. But being the chronic procrastinator that I am, I waited until eleven thirty. Of course, by this time I was in a mad rush to get out the door. I ran to my truck in the driveway and started it up. Now keep in mind that my truck was a twenty-two foot long, four-door pickup with a manual transmission, and our driveway was uphill from the road. As the truck warmed up, I remembered thinking, "Did I let the dogs in?" I couldn't remember, so out the truck I went, running to the backyard.

Sure enough, my two black labs, Pepper and Jack, sat there wagging their tails at me from the other side of the fence. I hurriedly hopped the fence and let them in the back door to the house. I knew I was going to be late for work, so I darted around the house to my driveway. As I rounded the garage, my truck was gone! A thought instantly raced through my head—someone saw it running and...but before I could even finish my thought, I noticed the truck just sitting in the middle of my street, blocking traffic. "Oh #^$%#," I thought to myself. I didn't set the parking brake.

Now my street wasn't the busiest street in the world, but there was a fair amount of traffic, and cars were stopped in the road on both sides of my truck. I remember fearing the worst and thinking that the truck rolled down the driveway uncontrollably and hit a poor kid on a bike, or a mom walking her baby, or the elderly gentleman that made his daily trek around the block. *Oh man, did I screw up!*

I ran down to the street, anxious and embarrassed, and when I got to the front of my truck, I timidly walked to the back to see what I had done. I saw some brownish-red fluid around the back tire, and my heart nearly stopped. Peering around the bumper simultaneously answered my prayers and calmed my fears. The back axle had bumped into a small boulder in my neighbor's yard and a brake line was severed, accounting for the leaking fluid.

Thankfully, no one was injured (or worse) and there was no damage to anything except my brakes, unless you count my ego. I solemnly climbed into the driver's seat and pulled back up the driveway to let the other vehicles by.

Call this situation what you will: fate, luck, coincidence, or an angel on my shoulder. No matter what you call it or how you view it, this was and always will be a situation for which I will be eternally thankful. I am grateful my life did not change that day in the negative ways it certainly could have. I choose to remember the gift I was given that day (among countless others I have received), during good times in my life and especially during the rough patches.

I'm sure you have many instances where you felt lucky or blessed; days when your life could have changed in almost inconceivable ways. Take a few minutes and think about those times right now and write them down on the following page.

<u>Situations in life where you felt extremely blessed/lucky:</u>

_____

_____

_____

_____

_____

_____

_____

_____

_____

_____

_____

_____

_____

_____

_____

_____

_____

_____

_____

_____

_____

_____

_____

_____

_____

_____

_____

_____

_____

_____

...dealing with adversity gets easier as time passes.

Look back at an occasion in your life when you were in a great deal of physical pain. Perhaps you suffered an injury or had an operation. At the time, the pain may have felt unbearable, but somehow you managed to get through it. Can you recall feeling the pain to the same degree and intensity that you felt while actually going through the situation? Probably not. Of course, you may remember the ordeal as being painful, but the point to understand here is that it no longer affects you in the same way—it does not hurt to the same degree.

Suffering from physical pain is similar to experiencing tragedy, hardship, or loss. The first days, months, and even years can seem unbearable. However, with time and a thankful outlook, pain will subside. Remember to view life in the biggest possible picture and maintain trusting faith. Make your outlook a positive, thankful one to the best of your ability, and your tough, trying, or tragic times will not affect you in the same way.

self-pity

Wallowing in self-pity is easy to do when you forget or ignore the fact that adversity will settle on every life. Everyone has worrisome problems or troubles, and at times, life can certainly be difficult; there is no question about that. Many people think they have grave problems, but the fact of the matter is most of us do not. When we compare our problems to some of the real tragedies in our world, we soon realize our troubles are often a by-product of a selfish perspective.

I have come to know an older couple who provide a good example of feeling pity instead of thankfulness. They were healthy all their lives, worked hard, and earned a good living that provided enough money to purchase a nice house, put food on the table, and still have some money in the bank. However, as sickness and general old age set in, they seemed to forget their many, many blessings.

In the process of dealing with their present situation, they chose to see only the immediate problems and pain that confronted them, and forgot about their blessings of health, prosperity, and a happy family. They failed to maintain a thankful view by not recognizing the absolute bounty received over the years.

If this couple were to look back on their lives with an attitude of gratitude, they would feel blessed for being healthy the majority of their lives, as well as for a healthy family. Sure, the pain would exist, and age would still take its toll; but a perspective of thankfulness would allow them to better cope with their current situation and empathize with what others are going through, instead of becoming increasingly withdrawn, jealous, and embittered.

Thankful perspective: Try not to pity yourself because of your circumstances; be happy your situation is not worse. If you are going through a tough time, do not compare your pain and suffering to the blessings others may be receiving. Be thankful for your life, empathetic to the trials people go through, and happy for others when good fortune embraces them.

Everyone will face tough times at some point, and feeling slighted seems normal only when you do not have a thankful perspective. In fact, it is indeed easy to pity yourself when you are selfishly preoccupied with what you *think* belongs to you. Self-pity is a negative characteristic that can be erased with a genuine perspective of gratitude.

worry, worry, go away!

Another major obstacle to being thankful is the human need to feel in control. People can be overcome with worry and speculation very easily when they don't realize just how much of life is out of the realm of personal control. While there are variables and situations that can be managed, such as how hard we work, how much effort we put into life, and the choices we make, ultimately we control very little. How many times have you or someone you know planned for a certain outcome and everything went awry? Situations are often out of our hands and circumstances can easily spiral out of our control.

Concern and care (a.k.a. worry) have a place and purpose, but excessive or misplaced worrying brings about negative thoughts and perspectives. This negativity entangles itself into all aspects of your life like a cancer and affects everything from health to interactions with others to success.

Many years ago, I was involved with a wedding that was meticulously scheduled. Every detail was planned, re-planned, and then thought about some more. Did I mention that this wedding was thoroughly planned? The soon-to-be newlyweds were trying the patience and kindness of everyone helping them prepare for the big event by getting a little obsessive about the whole production. The young couple would not stand for anything out of place. By focusing narrowly on their particular wants and wishes, they became unnecessarily anxious and angry, generating feelings of nervousness, stress, and anger toward each other as well as family and friends.

Following months and months of planning, the big day arrived. After extracting every bit of energy and goodwill from themselves and those around them, the bride and groom were set. A few hours before the wedding was to start, the groom's father went on a last-minute errand. As the clock ticked closer to the wedding hour, he had not returned and everyone started to get understandably anxious. The time for the ceremony to start passed…fifteen minutes…forty minutes…an hour went by. Regrettably, the wedding party received the unwelcome news that the groom's father had suffered a massive heart attack and was in intensive care at a local hospital. All the meticulous details of the wedding that caused so much anxiety and angst became unimportant. Thankfully, the father recovered and some very important life-lessons were learned that day.

Thankful perspective: Strive to not worry so much about trying to control life that you forget what is important. Losing sight of what you really have power over and becoming too involved with the details of life is a recipe for a rude awakening. Adversity finds everyone at some point and in some way; granted, a wedding can be a most stressful time, and this particular wedding scenario may be an extreme example, but try to keep your sense of control in check regarding details and situations in life. We can prepare for situations and plan for the future responsibly and carefully, but worrying about what is beyond our control causes unnecessary stress and obscures a thankful perspective.

Never let the future disturb you. You will meet it, if you have to,
with the same weapons of reason, which today arm you against the present.

–Marcus Aurelius

Learn to let go of the uncontrollable aspects of life and pour that energy into being grateful in thought, attitude, and action. Most of us are continually and constantly blessed throughout our lives. Let's try to remember that and give thanks.

Maintain a Thankful Perspective

As you incorporate thankfulness into your life and remove obstacles that hinder it, you can actively practice methods and trains of thought to help it take root and remain strong. Remember, your perception of life can allow you to find peace of mind and fulfillment regardless of what comes your way.

a thankful checklist

The everyday things in life are easily taken for granted. In order to change this, it is essential to recognize and be thankful for them as often as you can. I know it is impossible to feel thankful 100 percent of the time, and everyone is guilty of taking things for granted, but establishing and reflecting on an '*I am thankful for:*' checklist or gratitude journal can help you strengthen your perspective. Simply make a checklist of all you are grateful for in life. Keep a copy close to your hand as well as your heart. Inventory the contents of your list frequently, and constantly find more to add to it. Make it a habit to review your thankful checklist daily.

First, be thankful for waking. Feel blessed to have another day—not just a day for you and your loved ones, but be grateful the world has another sunrise. Now, if you can feel, give thanks. Can you hear? Can you see? Can you move at all? Can you think with a clear mind? If you answered yes to just one of these questions, be thankful. If you can say yes to more than one, consider yourself truly blessed.

Be grateful every day for your health. If you are not healthy in some aspects today, you can be thankful for the times you were healthy and for current health in other areas. The same goes for your loved ones. Are your loved ones well now or have they had health at one time? Do not forget these times simply because they may be gone—give thanks for them. Review your list often and let thoughts of thankfulness permeate your mind. Over time, they will serve to strengthen an attitude of gratitude and work magic with your perspective.

that's life

Challenging circumstances and down right awful things can happen to anyone at any time—life can be turned upside-down and changed forever in an instant. Difficulties and hardships fall upon everyone, as we go through trials, tribulations, and moments of negativity, each in our own time. However, the good news is that you can successfully deal with adversity by living with an attitude of gratitude and remaining thankful.

Life simply may not turn out exactly as you want it to…that *is* life. When adversity comes to rest on you in some way, be prepared. So many times I've heard people say, "I never thought this could happen to me," but the reality is such that something adverse can happen at any time. Of course, you shouldn't spend time worrying about the many bad things that could happen, but be willing to accept the fact that you are not immune from difficulties or tough, tragic times.

All too often, we don't realize what we have until strong adversity is bearing down on us. If you are facing real tragedy, try to remember what life was like before you were presented with serious problems. Do you look at others who are complaining about trivial or petty problems and tell yourself, "If I only had your problems?" Learn to view petty problems and inconveniences for what they truly are by remembering life could always be worse.

Life can seem rough and unfair, but as my grandma, Busia always told me, "The sun can't shine every day." There is much wisdom in that statement. Clouds and rain are just as important to our lives as the sun. Similarly, we need troubling times in life so we can learn from them, grow from them, and appreciate our good times more because of them. Difficult times ultimately prove to be as necessary to life as the good ones.

Life can be hard, but life happens. Cope with it as best you can while being thankful and fostering goodness. Do not be afraid of adversity, and try not to complain too much. That's life—give thanks for it.

thankfulness can be achieved

If it seems impossible to maintain an attitude of gratitude in your situation, remember that many people are inspiring examples of being able to do so during the most dire and dark circumstances imaginable. Interestingly, those who maintain a thankful perspective when tragedy strikes stand out like a lighthouse to a ship that is miles from shore.

I noticed one example of this while I was attending the funeral of a young child. The boy's grieving father was obviously distressed and sad, but he was the first to point out how thankful he was for the time he was given with his child. He did not pity himself because his wife passed away in a car accident a year earlier, nor he did pity himself through this very tough ordeal. He was grieving, of course, but stayed focused on the fact that nothing in life was truly his, and maintained strong faith. This perspective helped him remain thankful throughout his ordeal.

Another instance of achieving a perspective of gratefulness during unbearable circumstances starts with a family driving on the highway. Mom, Dad, and their four children were in the car. In the blink of an eye, a horrible accident caused an explosion to tear through the back of the vehicle. All four children perished in the flames. The parents survived, suffering an unbearable loss. They endured a grief few people will ever experience. Over time, the parents were able to be thankful for their children. They were hurt and grieving, but they were also able to trust in something greater than the here and now and put their hurt and pain and hope into their faith. Amazingly, years later, they are effectively coping and continuing with a purposeful, grateful life.

A third example of thankfulness brings us to a town that had just been ravaged by a tornado. Local news crews were interviewing area residents. One newscaster approached a woman who was in hysterics. Her husband and child were standing next to her, offering comfort and support as she wept.

"How could this happen?" she sobbed uncontrollably. "This is why we moved to this part of the country! Now we have nothing! Nothing!" Fortunately, she did not lose her family and no loved ones were hurt, but she was understandably distraught nonetheless.

The newscaster moved to another woman across the street. Her family was safe, and she lost all of her possessions in the storm as well. However, this woman held a strong perspective of thanks. The first words she spoke were, "Thank God my family is okay. It is only by the grace of God that we are still here. I know many other people are not so lucky, and my heart goes out to them."

The difference a thankful perspective can make is astounding. Two different people suffered similar losses, yet one perceives she lost everything, while another believes she has been given everything. The power of your perception is truly immense...take control of it and use it to feed that good wolf.

A final example of positive thankfulness comes from some of my best friends, Dawn and Gary. They are a married couple who bring warmth, friendliness, and positive energy wherever they go. They put the needs of others first as much as possible, but there came a day when Dawn and Gary had to put themselves first—but not for a selfish reason—Gary was diagnosed with cancer. That news would be enough to knock the wind out of anyone's sails, but despair was not an option.

Even though they had a two-year-old son and infant twin boys, Dawn and Gary faced this challenge head-on, with resounding faith, a thankful perspective, and an unshakable positive attitude. Smiles never ceased, laughter was always in the air, and their overwhelmingly positive character served to lift not only their spirits, but the spirits of those around them as well. The positive energy of their attitude worked wonders in all directions.

Fortunately, as of this writing, Gary and his family are winning the fight against the scourge of cancer. They know many trials are ahead, but their trusting faith and positive perspective of thankfulness remain unwavering. Ultimately, those things will help them get through any tough and trying times. I admire and respect their strength beyond words and look to the example they set in action and attitude as the thankfulness benchmark each of us should aspire to reach.

We all know of situations that are incredibly trying, because millions of examples of tragedy exist. Along with those tragedies and the tough times that go with them are positive examples of people maintaining thankful attitudes. Naturally, it isn't easy to feel grateful in extremely painful situations of tragedy and loss. However, get inspired by the examples of gratitude that are all around, because you can do it, too!

give thanks...literally

Life is a learning process. We can choose to learn from every experience or wallow in pity and be thankless when life does not turn out as we plan. At times, we experience much pain, both perceived and real, but we must keep the faith. Always feel a sense of gratitude for the past and present, no matter what comes along.

As your thankful perspective becomes stronger, you will learn to readily accept the fact that nothing is truly yours—every part of life is just a loan, a lease that can be rescinded at any time. Achieving this perspective gives you the strength that comes from knowing you no longer can lose anything when faced with adversity and hardship, because you understand that all in life is given to you.

Even though life can be painful, even unbearable at times, I believe we will eventually understand why. When people ask why bad things to happen or why senseless violence occurs in our world every day, remember, we are not privy to understanding the biggest picture. A true perspective of thankfulness allows you to have faith in something greater for all that happens in life, while giving you strength and courage.

Care for your needs, plan for and live your life, but always maintain an attitude of gratitude. If you have been blessed with health, opportunities, and the ability to accomplish, remember to *give* thanks. You can literally *give* thanks by sharing love, kindness, tolerance, and compassion. You can also give money, time, or service. Remember, those things are not yours in the first place—they are gifts to you. Do not be greedy with what you have, and give while you are able...*practice giving.*

☑ Action List: Look Up, Be Thankful

☒ Be thankful for each new day:
❑ Remember that every day is a gift—for you personally, as well as for the world.

☒ Are there some tragedies or hardships that you have undergone and become stronger because of them?
❑ Use your experience as a foundation for helping someone else going through challenging situations.

☒ Be thankful for your health:
❑ Remember that health is ultimately not in your hands.

☒ Be thankful for your abilities:
❑ Realize your abilities are gifts.
❑ Be humble.

☒ Remove obstacles that hinder a thankful perspective.

☒ Stop taking things for granted:
❑ Consciously think about and be grateful for what is in your life.
❑ Show gratitude in thought as well as action.
❑ Recognize that you are not entitled to health, happiness, or a good life—they are gifts.
❑ Be thankful for and humbled by the gifts you receive.

⊠ **Be willing to accept that adversity may strike at any time.**

⊠ **Be thankful through tough times:**
- ❑ Always find something to be thankful for, no matter what situation you are going through.
- ❑ Find thankful ways to deal with tough situations.

⊠ **Do not pity yourself because of circumstances in life:**
- ❑ View life with thankfulness instead of pity.
- ❑ Do not compare your problems with the problems of others.
- ❑ Remember, your situation could always be worse.
- ❑ View adversity as something that will make you stronger.
- ❑ Be happy for others when good fortune embraces them.

⊠ **Try not to worry about what cannot be controlled:**
- ❑ Much of life is beyond your control.
- ❑ Do not get so caught up with the details of life that you forget to act with thankfulness and goodness.
- ❑ Convert the energy spent on worrying into thankful thoughts and actions.

⊠ **Strengthen your thankful perspective.**

⊠ **Fill in your '*I am thankful fo*r': checklist:**
- ❑ Reflect on and write down everything you should be thankful for, from a new day, to health, to the goodness of humanity.

❏ Review your checklist several times a day and add to it often.

❏ Establish a routine for daily gratitude.

☒ Maintain an attitude of gratitude to the best of your ability:

❏ Take heart in the fact that people have gone through terrible situations and have been able to maintain a thankful perspective. So can you!

❏ Share some of the gifts you receive with others.

❏ Remember that a life clouded with selfishness cannot maintain a thankful perspective.

☒ Couple your thankful perspective with thankful actions of goodness.

I am thankful for:

1. _____
2. _____
3. _____
4. _____
5. _____
6. _____
7. _____
8. _____
9. _____
10. _____
11. _____
12. _____

Please add more to this list...

6

I, me, my, & mine...
from selfish to selfless

Only a life lived for others is a life worthwhile.

—Albert Einstein

Living in more positive, caring, and selfless ways drastically improves our lives and benefits everyone and everything around us; of that, there is no doubt. This certainly begs the question: *Why don't we do it more often?* In everyday life, being selfless can admittedly be a struggle. Even though we inherently know being selfless is a moral, virtuous, and right thing to do, we can often fail to live up to our full potential in that regard. There are many reasons why we choose to be selfish; we may have forgotten how to be selfless, or maybe haven't even considered it. In the end however, it is one of the most important things we can do with our lives.

Living selflessly is not a new idea; unfortunately, it often seems to be ignored or placed on the back burner. People can be so busily involved with their lives, troubles, and wants/needs that even accommodating the smallest actions of selflessness can become difficult. Without those small considerations, hope inevitably wanes for selfless thoughts and actions on a grander scale. This all but formally invites excessive negativity into the picture, leading to a downward spiral that affects individuals, families, organizations, and even entire countries in damaging and destructive ways.

Changing or reversing the effects of that downward spiral is such an enormous task that you may find it quite easy and natural to rationalize and justify that we are helpless to affect change on our own. After all, what can one person do to stem the tide of selfishness in our world? The answer to that question is very hopeful and powerful. When you live with selflessness, tiny seeds of goodness are planted. These seeds grow subtly, but they also take root deeply and grow exponentially. A little selflessness goes a long way toward bringing our world back to good, and each of us can help in the effort.

Although an innate knowledge of goodness exists within every person, the reality is that many of us struggle to truly connect with it. I know I can find it quite challenging at times to distinguish the difference between what is genuinely good and what is good for my selfish needs and desires. Personal views and opinions can easily become self-serving and conditional. By selfishly caring for physical, spiritual, material, and emotional needs, we can forget or even intentionally ignore the fact that other people require fulfillment of their own.

In today's world, perhaps more than ever, selfishness, ignorance, and intolerance can cause us to believe our own experience of life, such as certain spiritual beliefs, racial or social groups, nationality, personal perspectives, or culture is superior. While it is indeed healthy to feel pride and a connection to that which is important to you, problems develop when differences, no matter how innocent or benign, become objects of intolerance. This predicament runs the gamut from countries waging war to people committing crimes and violence, to the smaller, selfish interactions of people on an individual basis. Even something as seemingly insignificant as cutting in front of someone in line, giving a rude gesture while driving, or making fun of someone detracts from goodness in the same way, although not to the same degree, as more selfish, violent, or immoral actions.

Though many of us are taught to be selfless by family, religious/spiritual teachings, and friends, we often think and behave more selfishly than we should. While some degree of selfishness is necessary for survival, it can be taken beyond that original, positive intent; ranging from having petty arguments or difficulties with those around us, to phenomenal amounts of greed, jealousy, violence, and self-centeredness.

looking within...selfish to selfless

Do you think you are selfish? Do you know you are and honestly admit, "It's all about me," and believe that's okay? Oftentimes, any type of giving, sharing, or patience beyond personal needs can be a challenge. However, you have the ability to choose to be the working definition of positive or negative, to live with selflessness or to be selfish. If you elect the latter, you are choosing to bring intolerance, greed, jealousy, and a host of other bad intentions and situations into our world. On the other hand, deciding to be selfless by giving to others and fostering kindness, tolerance, and goodness brings happiness and peace.

In order to understand where you stand with regard to selfishness and selflessness in your life, it's important to delve deep into daily habits, routines, and thoughts to see what needs work...where you really need to improve. In addition to that, asking others who know you well can open your eyes to what may need changing. To start, look at your life thoroughly and ask...

- Am I as kind or courteous as I could be?
- Do I become angry quickly or find my patience wears thin easily?
- Are slight inconveniences blown out of proportion and handled in a selfish manner?
- Am I as selfless as I could be?
- Am I able to objectively view myself and find room for improvement?
- How elaborate do my material possessions need to be?
- Do I look down on others?
- Am I intolerant or envious of others?

Think about these questions and add more of your own. Prepare yourself to be willing to accept the fact that you may have some work to do in order to become more selfless. Like every living thing, we must focus on our needs in order to survive, but unlike other creatures, we have the ability to differentiate between what we want and what we need. Often, we know what we need, but may still want excessively beyond that point. Your thoughts and actions are personal choices, so no one can make them, correct them, or account for them except you. In order to get back to good, acknowledge and become aware of your selfish tendencies.

Following are some general definitions for selflessness and selfishness

We all fit somewhere between the extremes of being purely selfless and purely selfish, and regardless of the different circumstances you encounter that make your life unique, there is always room for improvement.

The following definitions are very
general and by no means all-inclusive.
Please add your insights to them.

defining selflessness

Selflessness is giving…pure and simple. There is one caveat however: The giving must be genuine—you give not to receive attention or expect something in return, but because you truly want to give from the bottom of your heart. Selfless acts range from being courteous while driving to giving donations; from volunteering time, to being friendly and kind, to taking the first steps in order to repair broken relationships.

Selfless people give as freely to those they do not know as they do to their loved ones, colleagues, and acquaintances. They will not judge based on appearance, spiritual beliefs, race, or preconceived ideas or stereotypes, and offer respect and tolerance to everyone. They will not look down on others regardless of social, economic, or educational class because they choose to apply the fact that everyone is equal.

Genuinely selfless people are forgiving and readily offer apologies by not holding grudges and putting aside personal pride if it means helping someone or mending a broken relationship. Finally, selfless people are nice, approachable, warm, and friendly. They offer patience in situations where most people would become angry, and rather than becoming impatient, they offer encouragement. Kindness is always a companion to their giving, and recipients of their selflessness never feel something is owed.

My definition of selflessness:

_____

_____

_____

_____

_____

_____

_____

_____

_____

How I can live more selflessly;

Family_____

_____

Work/School,etc:_____

_____

Myself_____

_____

defining selfishness

Selfish people care about themselves to the exclusion of others, but this definition goes far beyond simple self-centeredness to encompass all selfish thoughts and behaviors. Selfishness encourages giving only for gain, caring exclusively for one's needs and excluding others. These things cause people to live in a clouded bubble, dealing exclusively with what pertains to them. Blindly going about their lives, thinking only of what benefits them, they choose not to see that being selfless is necessary and good. Rarely will they look outside their bubble, and when they do, their perceptions are as blurry and distorted as looking through a real bubble. Unfortunately, they never pop the bubble or find a way to give to others outside of it without expecting something in return.

As selfish people sit in their self-inflicted confines, a distorted view of reality affects every aspect of life. Self-centeredness causes them to become too close to their lives, material belongings, and problems, which often turn out to be mere inconveniences. This begins the '*it's all about me*' complex. Even if life is going well, they will find something wrong or a way to complain. If life happens to place some bumps in the road, their complaints turn into tantrums.

As selfishly-minded people gain more material possessions, success, perceived power, or status, they often want more, and are rarely satisfied or thankful for what they have. Their selfishness affects the lives of those around them negatively as they often treat others poorly, and may even look at others who have received a blessing, be it in family, money, or success, and go so far as to begrudge the recipient.

The selfish mind tends to think negatively, "No one should have anything if I don't. I should not be made to suffer, struggle, or do without unless everyone else shares the same fate." They cannot enjoy someone else's happiness and good fortune because they always want more for themselves. Instead of taking a thankful perspective, selfish people are trapped in a circle of negativity where they constantly worry about what others may be getting or have received. They feel shorted, cheated, and slighted by life, society, and other people.

A selfish mindset shows an amazing amount of intolerance, ranging from ignorance and impoliteness, to prejudice, spite, and hatred based on racial, social, educational, personal, or spiritual differences. This person may feel superior to others for superficial, egotistical reasons and often feels he or she has to tolerate people. When dealing with others, they may act aggressively and be condescending; because the selfish mind can have much brain but very little mind. Translation: a selfish person can be well-versed and successful in the practical areas of life, but may ignore the knowledge of how to treat others with goodness. Of course, selfish people will not see their own faults or mistakes, because for them, it truly is *all about me.*

<u>My description of selfishness:</u>

_____

_____

_____

_____

_____

_____

_____

_____

_____

_____

How I am selfish:

_____

_____

_____

_____

_____

_____

_____

_____

_____

Selfless/Selfish Levels

Now that general definitions of selflessness and selfishness have been established, we will begin organizing those definitions into different categories so you can assess your own placement. These are, of course, open to your personal interpretation, and merely general guideline:

1. Completely Selfless = Goodness
2. Generally Selfless = Givers
3. Selfishly Selfless = Givers and Takers
4. Selfish = Takers
5. Excessive / Evil Selfishness = Evil Takers

At one end of the scale lies the ideal goodness of complete selflessness, and the other end is the extreme of excessive, evil selfishness. Everyone thinks and acts in ways that put them at some point on the scale. Place yourself into the level or levels that best describe you. Once you have a point of reference, you can begin to work toward becoming more selfless. Remember, you may need objective opinions from people who know you in order to make an accurate placement.

1: Completely Selfless-Goodness

Complete selflessness is more of an ideal, rather than an attainable level of human ability. However, a small percentage of humanity manages to fit into this category by consistently sustaining a lifestyle that entails giving to others in thought, action, and attitude. They live for others, understanding and showing the true meaning of life: to give, to be helpful, to show tolerance and care, to offer forgiveness, and to live with goodness. Their thoughts and deeds are selflessly directed toward others, as well as the very nature that supports life. Selfish actions, beyond basic needs of survival, are non-existent.

2: Generally Selfless — Givers

This level describes people who consistently exemplify traits and actions that define selflessness. They offer help and encouragement to others in any capacity possible. While the vast majority of their thoughts and actions are selfless, emotions, feelings, and circumstances in life can cause this type of person to lose their way from selflessness from time to time, although very rarely. A person in this category would never intentionally hurt, harm, or cause pain. More than likely, people who truly belong in this category would not place themselves in it, as they always feel they could be more doing more to be selfless.

3: Selfishly Selfless — Givers & Takers

The vast majority of humanity belongs in this level, which contains aspects of selflessness and selfishness. People who fit in this level care for themselves and the needs and wants of others, but are not selfless to their full potential. They are well-meaning, good-natured, and caring people who simply do not live as selflessly as they could. At times, selfless thoughts and actions may only apply to those who are important to them, such as family and friends, while they show something less than selflessness toward others (or vice versa).

Selfishly selfless people can be judgmental and hurtful. Examples range from getting upset over the everyday situations of life to holding grudges; from maintaining a view of superior or exclusively righteous beliefs to showing slight amounts of prejudice toward those who are different. They may believe any perspective differing from theirs is incorrect, invariably resulting in some degree of intolerance and judgment. However, this person will never tolerate the extremes of hatred or violence.

On the flip side, they are selfless by giving to others, offering help, kindness, forgiveness, and showing genuine concern and compassion. Remember, the majority of humanity fits somewhere into this level, with ample room for improvement.

4: Selfish — Takers

This category covers people who care exclusively for themselves. They often lead socially correct lives, function well in society, and become materially successful by caring for what is important to them. However, everything in life is "all about them." They only look for ways to benefit themselves, protect what is theirs, and do not care for the needs, feelings, or wishes of a person who is outside their perspective.

A selfish person does not consider giving to others for the sake of goodness, and can be intolerant and judgmental. If your beliefs are not like theirs, then you are wrong. If you are not in the same social, racial, or educational class, they will look down on you, be intolerant, or try to degrade you for your differences. Selfish people maintain perspectives of superiority and choose not to acknowledge the fact that people are fundamentally equal.

5: Extreme Selfishness — Evil Takers

Those who care exclusively for themselves and break laws of humanity, society, and goodness in order to get what they desire fall into this category. They will use force, violence, deceit, or evil, heinous, or atrocious actions in order to satisfy their wants. People who fit in this level do not care how their actions will affect others. They lack and/or ignore any sense of right and wrong, do not have remorse about any harm committed, and are not affected by conscience. True spirituality is non-existent in their lives. Any perceived spirituality or connection to goodness is grossly distorted from reality (i.e. to kill in the name of a particular belief or inflict harm on others because they are not of the same faith, race, nation, social class, etc.).

Only a relatively small percentage of humanity fits into this category. That fact may be hard to accept because of the preponderance of negativity reported in the media, but out of the billions of people inhabiting our world, only a minuscule number actually fall into this category. Unfortunately, evil actions, and the people who commit them, get inordinate amounts of attention.

Where do you fit?

Take a good, honest look.

You may find that you fit into several categories due to the many different situations and dynamic circumstances you come across on a daily basis. You may have a more selfish perspective than you realize, so your assessment may not be entirely accurate. Again, ask people who know you well to objectively and candidly describe your traits and tendencies. Try not to get angry or defensive about their views, but consider their comments as tools for you to make a proper assessment, ultimately helping you become more selfless.

Honest criticism is hard to take, particularly
from a relative, a friend, an acquaintance, or a stranger.

–Franklin P. Jones

Just as the quote alludes to, hearing criticism is not a very easy thing to do. However, assess your thoughts and actions, past and present, and take a close look at yourself. Maybe you are not as tolerant as you should be. For instance, does race or physical appearance play a role in how you view a person? Are you tolerant of other spiritual or religious beliefs, or think your views are exclusively correct? There are also other avenues available to explore by asking...

- Do I gossip?
- Am I jealous of the possessions, lifestyle, or accomplishments of others?
- Am I selfless only with loved ones, but not toward other people (or vice versa)?
- Do I outwardly show selflessness, but think the opposite?
- Am I easily upset in situations that require patience?
- Am I judgmental?
- Do apologies, forgiveness, and thankfulness flow easily from my mind as well as my mouth?

Take an objective look and find areas to improve.

become selfless

After identifying problem areas, make a list of your selfish thoughts and actions—don't forget the small things. Draft a plan to correct selfish tendencies by writing down what you can do in order to change and promptly put that plan into action. Remember, moving toward selflessness is a process that takes effort and time. Start small and be consistent in your approach.

Simple daily actions, such as smiling and saying hello to someone walking by or being genuinely nice to others are a great start. You can hold a door for someone, be patient while driving, offer an apology, and make the first call to repair a relationship. Say thank you. Hold your temper. Give of yourself in any number of different ways to people you know, as well as to those you don't. Giving selflessly can be accomplished by sharing kindness, forgiveness, tolerance, patience, time, encouragement, compassion, and material help, to name just a few.

Many people consider themselves to be selfless, but they can be quick to balk or stop short when an opportunity to be kind or giving to others is presented to them. They may have difficulty extending even the smallest actions of selflessness, such as leaving a generous tip at a restaurant, saying thank you, being tolerant, or showing kindness and patience in everyday actions with family and friends. They can be self-centered regarding faith and forget that true spirituality demands goodness, selflessness, and tolerance.

Do not let this become the case for you. Be less concerned with telling others how selfless you are and let your actions be your voice. Small measures of selflessness are just as important as grand ones, because they are an important part of the foundation for becoming a better person.

When you wander from the path of goodness (and we all will), your selfless acts can lose value. For instance, if someone gives to you in some way, yet treats you badly in other situations, their selfless acts can lose value. Therefore, it is especially important to be as consistent as possible with selfless behaviors. Of course, there will be times when you fall short and make mistakes—being selfless is not always easy, but if you wander from the path, be sure to find your way back.

Success consists of getting up
just one more time than you fall.

-Oliver Goldsmith

only judge your self...*ishness*

Many people self-righteously label those who are well off in some area of life as being selfish. Who is able to draw the distinction between what is too much and just enough as it pertains to lifestyle or possessions? For example, a person who earns an average wage and owns a modest house may believe a person with a substantial home has "too much." To that person, "too much" may mean someone who owns lavish houses on two continents, a 225-foot yacht, and other materialistic luxuries. However, to someone struggling to put food on the table and pay the rent, a person with a modest house may seem to have "too much." Finally, a person who has given up most of his or her worldly possessions to selflessly help others may view everyone who does not give to that same degree as having "too much." This begs the question: Who can definitively judge what is considered too much?

How much does one person need? Only that one person can honestly answer this question. No one has the right to judge what is too much or incorrect regarding material possessions or lifestyles, as long as no hurt or harm is caused. You may express what would be correct for yourself, but material possessions and lifestyle, as long as they cause no hate, harm, or intolerance, are a matter of perspective and personal choice. (That's not to say those choices are spiritually or morally correct; I am merely pointing out that you and I do not have the right to judge.) Every person is responsible for deciding his or her own actions, and every individual is ultimately held accountable for those actions. Again, do not judge others—apply that judgment to yourself and choose to find more goodness in your life.

Do not automatically stereotype an individual as being selfish simply because of financial means. Wealth, in and of itself, is not necessarily an indicator of selfishness—actions toward others are. A person who is well off financially can be as kind, generous, and giving as a person who has means that are more modest. Indeed, people of modest means can be as stingy, self-centered, and selfish as the night is dark. Learn to look at a person's attitude and actions instead of looking at what he or she owns.

***

Having a selfless attitude is far more important than wealth or material possessions.
***

Concern yourself with *your* choices instead of judging the actions and possessions of others. Ultimately, you will justify and account for your thoughts, actions, and lifestyle—no one else's. Try to live with more selflessness and tolerance, instead of passing judgment. While it may be difficult for you to recognize selfish thoughts and behaviors, do not let this discourage you—let it motivate you to learn how to recognize and shun selfishness.

Any selfless act, whether giving something you own, offering a nice gesture, or being tolerant, will expand and grow exponentially as it touches the lives of others. A single act of selflessness, done for the sake of goodness, will give rise to more good thoughts and deeds. Everyone you meet can be inspired in such beneficial ways that the overall positive effects are nearly impossible to imagine. Become selfless to the best of your ability.

☑Action List: Selfish to Selfless

☒ Learn to identify and shun selfishness:
❏ Identify selfish thoughts and behaviors, large and small.
❏ Do not rationalize that you are not selfish simply because you have not broken any laws or committed significant actions of selfishness.
❏ Recognize that selfishness covers everything from intolerance, to stealing, to making fun of someone, to judging others.

☒ Selfishness can be changed:
❏ Foster goodness by replacing selfishness with selflessness.

☒ Make a personal to-do list to encourage selflessness.

☒ Assess your thoughts and actions:
❏ Get an objective opinion to help you identify your strengths and weaknesses.
❏ List your selfish behaviors, make a plan, and commit to become selfless.

☒ Be selfless to the best of your ability.

☒ Do not judge others with respect to their possessions or lifestyle, as long as no hurt or harm is caused:
❏ Recognize that everyone is accountable for his or her own lifestyle and actions.

7

practice giving

You make a living by what you get,
but you make a life by what you give.

—Winston Churchill

The act of giving transforms selfless thoughts and aspirations directly into action. To give, in the truest sense of the word, means to do so for the sake of giving and extending goodness…not to expect something in return. True giving stems from knowing in your heart that it is the right thing to do. As the keeper of your love, kindness, and tolerance, as well as your positive attitude of gratitude and patience, you have the responsibility to give those things. Share them often and freely. Also, helping others, caring for nature, and offering forgiveness, as well as giving gifts of your compassion, empathy, time, money, and encouragement are more ways to give. While it is true we cannot be involved in everything that occurs in our family, community, or world, most of us are able to direct a larger part of our time and energy toward giving in some way.

The extent to which you give makes little difference on the scales of goodness. The important thing is for you to give genuinely. An authentic intention far outweighs what you actually give. For instance, if you are only able to donate a small amount of money or time, do not fret—give what you can when you can, because *the act of giving* is what's important

give tolerance

No one is born hating another person because of the color of his skin, or his background, or his religion. People must learn to hate; and if they can learn to hate they can be taught to love, for love comes more naturally to the human heart than its opposite.

-Nelson Mandela

Human beings naturally feel comfortable with people and things that are familiar to them. That being said, we should be very tolerant of one another despite our superficial differences because we are essentially the same. Our meager genetic differences are what give us variations in skin color, height, and other physical characteristics. Add to these our cultural, spiritual, and personal distinctions, and we become unique individuals; but those differences simply cannot be justification for intolerance. The common bonds we share are much more evident and powerful.

No human being has the right to dictate what should be tolerated regarding beliefs, characteristics, lifestyles, or perspectives, as long as those things do not promote hatred or harm. Simply because a person is different from you in some way does not give you the right or justification to be intolerant of that diversity. By the same token, do not feel superior or better than someone else because of differences. There are many ways to live and express ourselves, and as long as no hurt or harm is caused, each one is as valid as the next. After all, the beauty and glory of our world stems from the very diversity that it nurtures.

Intolerance encompasses everything from disliking someone because of looks, such as race, dress, or physical stature, to being narrow-minded or prejudiced against a person's beliefs, lifestyle, or personality. Intolerance does not have to be outwardly expressed to be hurtful, and it can affect your outlook and attitude by causing selfishness and negativity to be expressed through your words and actions—even if you are not consciously aware of it.

Everyone comes from the same source. If you hate another human being, you're hating part of yourself.

–Elvis Presley

Every person has distinctive viewpoints and opinions resulting from unique beliefs, life experiences, and personality. While your views, perspectives, and opinions are correct and true for you, they are not necessarily the best or most righteous, simply your own. Problems develop when people think their views are superior or exclusively correct and try to force them onto others. This is exemplified by what I like to call the '*I'm the only one who knows how to drive* syndrome.'

Driving is a most useful example for demonstrating the self-centeredness and intolerance of people, because it so readily brings out undesirable tendencies. There is nothing like getting behind the wheel of a car to bring out impatience, selfishness, anger, self-righteousness, and intolerance; but the principles demonstrated can apply to every aspect of life.

"I'm the only one who knows how to drive."

When driving, people tend to only see *their* immediate needs and no one else's. For instance, do you find yourself thinking other travelers do not need to get where they are going as badly as you do? Or, do you feel that their right to be on the road is not as important as yours? You have to do what you have to do in order for you to get to where *you* are going, right? Do you see a pattern here?

Syndrome Example 1: Imagine you are in a hurry, but the car in front of you is going the speed limit or perhaps a little faster. Does that driver's "slow driving" begin to irritate you? Do you start tailgating the car, thinking, "C'mon! Can't you see I'm in a hurry? SPEED UP!" After a stoplight or stop sign, you may think the driver is taking an extraordinarily long time to get going—just to tick you off.

Now, anger and intolerance have entered the picture. That person could drive faster! After all, with an intolerant, selfish perspective, *your* need to reach *your* destination is more important than another driver's right to observe the speed limit, because *your* needs come first. Think about why you are angry. What is the other person doing that's wrong?

How would you feel if you were treated with this same type of intolerance? Well, let's take a moment and turn the example around: You've had a rough day, and in order to relax and unwind, you plan to take a nice, leisurely ride home. You are traveling at the speed limit or perhaps a little faster when you notice a pair of headlights in the rearview mirror. The light becomes increasingly brighter as the car gets closer...and closer still. Finally, it is so close that a tap of your brake pedal would cause a collision. What is this driver doing? What a jerk! Some people are so impatient! Your right to drive the speed limit is more important than the tailgater's desire to get to his destination faster.

Do you remember the first part of the example? Is it okay if you are intolerant or impatient with someone else when it suits your needs, but not okay when those things are done to you? If you recognize yourself in these situations, take the opportunity to identify and address your actions and attitudes. Try on the other person's driving gloves and view things for a minute from his or her perspective.

Syndrome Example 2: This scenario starts when you are driving down the open road. Suddenly, someone turns in front of you. You have to slam on the brakes to avoid a collision. To top things off, the inconsiderate driver seems to be taking forever to get up to speed. You tailgate the bumper to make sure he knows you are upset and think, "That unbelievable "#@*&!@#$*^&% so-and-so!" Your blood pressure is up, you are upset, and the way you are driving unquestionably shows your anger. "What an inconsiderate driver! He is definitely wrong," you say (possibly with a little stronger language). While that may be true, you should remember to give that driver some space. "Why should I?" you may ask. "A driver should know better! This is my lane! That's unacceptable! A driver like that shouldn't be allowed on the road."

First of all, I think we all could relax…there is no reason to become upset, territorial, or impatient over petty things as quickly as many of us do. Everybody makes mistakes. Have patience. Be tolerant and understanding about the mistakes of others because you want and deserve that same tolerance for yourself—don't you? Learn to give people the benefit of the doubt and treat the shortcomings and mistakes of others with the same amount of tolerance you afford yourself.

Turn this second example around: If you were to pull out in front of someone thinking you had plenty of time to do so, but really didn't, you would undoubtedly appreciate another driver giving you some slack (tolerance). How would you feel if the driver you just cut off were to flash the bright lights and crawl up your bumper? Do *they* then become *the jerk*? Do you think, "Can't they understand? I thought I had more time. I just made an error in judgment! What an impatient "&^%#*!" In other words, do you give the same amount of patience and understanding to others that you afford yourself?

***

Apply these principles to every aspect of life and recognize your actions of intolerance. Give the same amount of patience, tolerance, and understanding to others that you want for yourself.

***

Now that you have had the opportunity to think about these scenarios, consider the following questions.

- Do I often blame *"They - Them - Him - Her – She – He - It?"*
- Is someone or something else always at fault?
- Do I notice everyone else has faults and makes bad mistakes?
- Do I dislike certain ways people treat me, only to turn around and act the same way?
- Am I able to find justification for my mistakes easily?
- Do I readily offer tolerance for the shortcomings of others?

Ask yourself these questions and answer them honestly. Ironically, the worst perpetrators of personal intolerance are often the most inept at dealing with intolerance aimed at them. Many of us can readily feel other people are often at fault, wrong, or misguided, and this is demonstrated when we are too critical of the shortcomings and mistakes of others, while forgetting or minimizing our own weaknesses and errors. You may think, "I don't make many mistakes or have many faults. Well, at least mine are not as bad as other peoples'." While your mistakes and faults may not seem so bad, remember that is because they do not seem so bad *to you.*

When you only have tolerance for yourself, you immediately become intolerant of others. If you tend to be critical of others, take those lenses of criticism you use to so deftly point out the faults and weaknesses of others and view yourself through them. You will see that you have just as many imperfections as everyone else. Accept the fact that you are no better than that person standing next to you. When you recognize this, you will find it harder to feel intolerant of others.

What is tolerance?
It is the consequence of humanity.
We are all formed of frailty and error;
let us pardon reciprocally each other's folly—
that is the first law of nature.
–Voltaire

spiritual tolerance

Spirituality is a very personal, deep-rooted issue, and discussing differing views often leads to intense debates, disagreements, or arguments. Spiritual convictions are often so strong and profound that many people can find it virtually impossible to tolerate and respect different outlooks. Nevertheless, living with goodness dictates that we become as tolerant as possible in every aspect of our existence, especially those concerning spiritual beliefs.

People naturally view things differently, but spiritual views can easily become selfishly skewed. Problems begin to surface when people try to force their convictions on others. Remember, just as there are many different languages, ways to set up governments, and the diverse cultures in our world, there can be many interpretations of religious and spiritual beliefs.

Focus your energy on what truly matters—connecting spiritually in order to foster goodness. If you express faith in your own way, it is important to allow others to express faith as it suits them. In order to become more tolerant, learn about and explore other views of faith. Countless belief systems, traditions, and perspectives can be valid as long as they do not promote hateful, intolerant, or harmful behaviors. You may not know about differing beliefs, or feel completely comfortable with other spiritual customs or views; but spiritual tolerance does not ask you to believe or worship differently, merely to believe what is right for you, live with a grateful heart, and treat others as you want to be treated.

become tolerant

Find ways to stem the tide of intolerance in your mind. If that includes the outward appearance of another person, remind yourself that others must tolerate the way you look. If you do not like the personality or beliefs of another person, remember, your personality and beliefs have to be tolerated by others as well. You simply do not have the right to be intolerant because of differences.

Can someone force you to stop being intolerant? The answer is no. That change must come from you. The choice to be open-minded regarding the many differences and diversities you face is yours alone. Be aware of the fact that if you take a tolerant view, there is no guarantee others will do the same for you. In the real world, intolerance will rear its ugly head in some form, but try to be a better person and show tolerance to the best of your ability.

give help

*In helping others, we shall help ourselves, for whatever
good we give out completes the circle and comes back to us.*

—Flora Edwards

There is a constant ebb and flow throughout the world regarding what people have, what people need, and what people have to give. We can be strong at times, yet weak or helpless under different circumstances. Out of that imbalance comes our responsibility and opportunity to help one another.

The ways we can help are as vast and varied as the number of people on Earth, because each of us can help uniquely. These range from giving time or money to being genuinely kind; from helping a troubled youth to showing compassion; from lending a sympathetic ear to adopting a child. Some people feel comfortable volunteering to benefit a specific cause, while others give by donating time or expertise through large organizations. Still others can help by writing a check, which is volunteering in a different way. No form of help is too big or too small.

When some aspects of life are going well, as when you may be enjoying good health, stable finances, or good cheer, share some of that good fortune by directing it toward others. If life is not going so well, try to give what you can, even if that is a smile—all means of giving are important.

While each person shares the responsibility to be helpful, we are not destined to give in the same way. Do not measure your gifts of help against the gifts of others; give to the best of *your* ability. Help may go to family members and people you come across daily, as well as to others you may not know in more distant places. Learn to offer help because you want to, because it fosters goodness, not because you expect to gain from it. Last but not least, do not brag about the help you have given or make a recipient of your helpfulness feel he or she owes you.

give forgiveness

*If we really want to love,
we must learn how to forgive.*

—Mother Teresa

To forgive is to let go; choosing to replace feelings of anger and hurt with the calmness and peace of mind forgiveness affords by changing negative feelings, emotions, and actions into positive thoughts and attitudes. Undoubtedly, there are times when forgiving is hard, but the benefits far outweigh any difficulties involved. Forgiveness can repair relationships, remove stress and negativity, and move you closer to goodness.

Over the course of life, every one of us will become hurt or angered by the words, thoughts, and actions of other people or by forces of nature. When you are hurt or angry, you engage a natural process to deal with those feelings. Becoming mad or detached from whomever or whatever has caused your pain is normal, but those feelings may turn into grudges and breed negativity in your attitude, well-being, and treatment of others.

The act of forgiveness is a great way to release negativity, but I'm sure you don't need me to tell you that it can be difficult. Pain can run so deep or be so scarring emotionally, that releasing a grudge and offering forgiveness may not come to mind readily or even at all. Remember, there are no timetables or specific steps you can take as a sure-fire way to hasten forgiveness, because subtle and major differences affect every situation and person uniquely.

Type I Forgiveness: forgive *and* forget: The defining characteristics of Type I Forgiveness allow you to harness its positive power and continue in a healthy, productive relationship with someone who may have hurt, offended, or harmed you. Many different factors can either help or hinder Type I Forgiveness, the most important of which is your attitude and ability to forgive. If you are a forgiving person by nature and can shrug off negativity quite easily, forgiving and forgetting will come naturally for you. However, if you have trouble letting go, you may have a tougher time. Also, there are extremely difficult circumstances and situations, which often cannot simply be forgiven and forgotten. In these cases, you will need to explore something different.

Type II Forgiveness: forgive to *keep moving forward*: Sometimes situations are so difficult, and your hurt, pain, and anger can be so devastating that forgiving and forgetting is virtually impossible. Perhaps the person who caused your pain is unwilling or unable to offer an apology or doesn't acknowledge any wrongdoing. Maybe you have lost contact, or the person has passed away. Type II Forgiveness can help you deal with situations involving other people, and it can also help you deal with circumstances and situations out of your control.

When forces of nature cause devastation, or when you or a loved one suffers physical illness, there is often no one for you to specifically blame, no one who can offer you an apology. By learning to forgive and let go, you will be able to focus on your positive attitude and responsibility for goodness. When forgiving *and* forgetting is not possible, forgiving to *keep moving forward* can help you work through the negativity that is sometimes inescapable in this life. Although you may not be able to forgive directly for any number of reasons, you are in effect forgiving by letting go of the negativity associated with certain situations. Type II Forgiveness allows you to move forward in a healthier, more positive way.

With your connection to goodness, your perspectives of thankfulness, and your selfless attitude, reflect on reasons why you should forgive, and try your best to do so. Pay particular attention to your thankful checklist and be grateful for what you have received. Even if you cannot forgive readily or completely, it is important to keep trying. Challenge yourself to be a better person by forgiving as much and as often as you can. Of course, you will not be able to forgive readily in every circumstance, but try your best.

Learning to let things go and forgive isn't
always easy, but when we truly forgive, it helps foster
better health, better relationships, a deeper sense of purpose
and self worth, and a feeling of connection to others.

–Robert Alan

Forgiving and releasing grudges forces negative emotions out of your mind so positive thoughts and feelings can help you foster goodness. There will be moments when other people do not understand what hurts you—sometimes they simply will not care. At other times, you will not get apologies or sincere explanations for many things that cause you pain. While people certainly cause problems, difficult situations can simply be an unpleasant fact of life.

When you have trouble forgiving, remember that you have done or will do things that offend, anger, or hurt others. If you desire forgiveness for your mistakes, forgive others as best you can. When you are able to forgive, be sure to offer it in a true and complete manner. Do not hastily claim you have forgiven someone and then hold it over that person's head or make those you have forgiven feel they owe you. The bottom line is to simply try your best…it can be hard, I know, but you will be better for having tried.

give apologies

An apology is the superglue of
life. It can repair just about anything.

–Lynn Johnston

Apologies can build bridges across gaps or faults in relationships and heal wounds that have been created. A true apology, by its very nature, shows you are sorry for what you have done, and just as importantly, that you do not intend to do the same thing again. When giving a sincere apology, it is important for you to understand that you have brought some kind of pain or offense to someone and should sincerely empathize with the hurt they feel. A true apology means you will try in earnest to stop the behavior or actions that necessitated the apology in the first place.

When you are the one who offends or causes pain, you must be the one to offer a heartfelt, sincere apology. If you have wronged someone, apologize. If a person believes you have wronged him or her, try to get to the source of the problem and offer an apology for any misunderstanding. This may not always be practical or plausible (indeed, I have instances in my own life where I am trying to do this), but it can work wonders to repair relationships and bring a positive energy and attitude to all involved. And remember, simply because something would not offend or hurt you, does not mean it cannot offend someone else. Be aware of what you say and do to others. If they are hurt by your words or actions, set aside your pride, apologize, and ask for forgiveness.

When you act in ways that are hurtful to others, the only way to correct the situation is to go to the person and admit what you have done was wrong. Then, offer a sincere apology. This is not simply lip service—it shows you understand and empathize with the hurt you have caused. Once you apologize, make every effort to stop the offending behavior. This step is a very important factor in repairing relationships and encouraging forgiveness. Complete forgiveness will become a more difficult process if the "wrongdoer" does not make a sincere apology.

give kindness

No kind action ever stops with itself. One kind action leads to another.
Good example is followed. A single act of kindness throws out roots in
all directions, and the roots spring up and make new trees. The greatest
work that kindness does to others is that it makes them kind themselves.

–Amelia Earhart

Giving is made whole when carried out with kindness, such as helping others in a caring, compassionate way, or by giving sympathy, forgiveness, and love. In other instances, kindness may be less obvious, but no less important; such as holding your anger in check—even if you have perceived the right to be angry, tempering your words to prevent an argument or backing down once one has started. Other ways to offer kindness include being polite to a person you do not really care for, expressing tolerance, and maintaining your composure and patience when dealing with the mistakes and shortcomings of others, as well as yourself.

Acts of kindness can occur when we simply change the way we face annoying, everyday situations. We can get irritated with people who can't control the very situations that cause us grief—usually they are just innocent bystanders. For instance, if you are at a crowded restaurant and your food takes a long time to arrive at the table, do you become angry and take it out on the server? Do you get upset at the technician who shows up to fix your internet connection because you are angry the line is in trouble? Do you become annoyed and intolerant of others in a crowded store even though you are a contributing factor to that crowd? Ask yourself if you should be getting angry with the people involved in these circumstances. Learn to re-direct and override your irritation or anger at situations or people who just happen to be around when you become annoyed.

Giving kindness will benefit you as much as the person who receives it because it brings peace and positivity to every situation, allowing people to act with reason and intellect instead of reacting with selfishness and negativity. Think of examples in life where you lose patience and get angry too quickly with people who do not deserve it. By truly listening, being tolerant, saying thanks, and being patient, you show kindness. Every kind action is grand because of the exponential potential for goodness that exists within it.

give environmentally

We do not inherit the Earth from our
ancestors, we borrow it from our children.

–Native American Proverb

Humankind has lived symbiotically with nature for millennia. Until relatively recently, that relationship has been successful. However, due to our many technical and industrial advances, the Earth is in throes of seemingly increasing pain. Nature's equilibrium is out of balance with signs that are evident now—today—but many dire problems will not be known for years to come.

We consume our natural resources at an alarming rate and continue to pollute and poison the very nature that sustains us. We necessarily live "in the now" to care for our needs, but must be more proactive about living for the future, so our grandchildren's grandchildren will be sustained by a healthy planet.

What can be done?

You can do many things to help. First, educate yourself on environmental issues and support those in the political and business arenas who combat the poisoning of our world. Take it upon yourself to learn about the hundreds of different things you can do to support and nurture the environment.

Every day you can take part with simple and easy actions such as recycling, preventing pollution, handling waste products properly, conserving energy and water, seeking renewable energy sources, incorporating environmentally friendly attitudes in your purchases, and reducing and reusing. Some easy things you can do are:

- Change your light bulbs to low energy bulbs.
- Recycle at home and at work or school.
(One guy at work calls me the cardboard cop!)
- Compost.
- Be water wise.
- Carpool, ride a bike, or walk whenever possible.
- Use rechargeable batteries.
- Buy paper goods made from recycled materials.

Now these are just a very few, simple possibilities of living a healthy, environmentally friendly lifestyle...for additional resources and/or information, please visit Earth911.org or MakeYourDifference.Org. We can only ignore the poisoning of our food and water and continue to consume natural resources at the current alarming rates for so long before our actions negatively affect everyone.

give simply…simply give

When you are willing to share with others, you have come to realize that life, and all that goes with it, is a blessing. The point is not how much you are able to give, the point is *to give*. Give of yourself because you truly want to help others and foster goodness. Give to others by nurturing our environment, offering help, and being tolerant and trusting. Offer patience and forgiveness. Listen to others and encourage with kindness.

I've learned that people will forget
what you said, people will forget what you did,
but people will never forget how you made them feel.

-Maya Angelou

Once you have gained the ability to give of yourself without expectation of getting something in return, you have mastered an important purpose for life—selflessness. Do not miss an opportunity to make someone's day, week, year, or life a bit more enjoyable by showing you care. Through selfless giving, you can change someone's life!

Take care of yourself and your loved ones, take time out when you need to, and when you are able to, give, give, and then give some more. Give in any way, to any degree. Life can be hard enough; don't make it more difficult by hindering goodness through negative thoughts and behaviors. Fulfill a major purpose of life by finding ways to give.

I am only one, but still I am one;
I cannot do everything, but still I can do something;
And just because I cannot do everything,
I will not refuse to do the something that I can do.

–Helen Keller

☑Action list: Giving

☒ Give personal tolerance:
❑ Do your best to tolerate unique viewpoints, lifestyles, and physical characteristics, as long as they do not cause hate or harm.
❑ Be as tolerant of the shortcomings of others as you are of your own.
❑ Do not force your views or opinions on others.

☒ Give spiritual tolerance:
❑ Do not force your spiritual views upon others.
❑ Practice tolerance by remembering your spiritual preference is not necessarily correct for everyone.

☒ Give help to others:
❑ Offering help is one of the best things you can do in life.
❑ Offer help in many different and unique ways.
❑ Do not miss an opportunity to help someone—you will need help someday.

☒ Give forgiveness to others:
❑ Replace feelings of hurt and anger by forgiving.
❑ Forgive as a means to release grudges that take away from your ability to foster goodness.
❑ Give Type II forgiveness to help you offer Type I Forgiveness.

☒ Give Kindness to others:
❑ Allow the natural trait of kindness to surface in your daily life.
❑ Every kind action is grand because of its potential for goodness.
❑ Give with kindness.

☒ **Give Environmentally:**
    ❑ Do not waste precious natural resources.
    ❑ Find ways to help our environment.

☒ **Create your own To-Do list—Giving.**

☒ **Remember, *giving* is good:**
    ❑ Giving fulfills you in fundamental ways that simply are not reachable by any other means.

My Goodness Campaign
Goals For Giving

Date:_____

❑**Tolerance:** _____

_____

_____

_____

❑**Help:** _____

_____

_____

_____

❑**Forgiveness:** _____

_____

_____

_____

❑**Kindness:** _____

_____

_____

_____

❑**Environmentally:** _____

_____

_____

_____

8

nurture your health

The greatest wealth is health.

–Virgil

Healthy attitudes, outlooks, and behaviors allow goodness to be encouraged and shared, and the quote from Virgil powerfully articulates this message: without health, life can certainly be difficult. Health is often taken for granted; while we have it, we may not give it a second thought, however, we quickly realize just how important a place being healthy occupies in our lives if we lose it.

As I mentioned earlier, health is ultimately out of our hands, but that's not to say we should wash our hands of taking care of ourselves, as we are responsible to be very involved with the aspects of health that are within our control. Take stock of your health by assessing and identifying where you need to change for the better. Once you find areas needing attention, take action. Remember, you do not have to do this alone or overnight—help is available from many different sources and can take time. You can seek support and guidance from friends, family, books, clubs, and health care professionals.

A good place to start in becoming healthier is to look at the habits you've developed and find out which ones are taking you to the right places and the ones that are unhealthy in every aspect of life.

Who am I?

I am your constant companion. I will push you forward to success or I will drag you down to failure. I am completely at your command. 80% of what you do, you might as well hand over to me, I will do it promptly, and I will do it correctly.

I am easily managed; you must merely be firm with me. Show me what you'd like to have done, and after a couple of lessons, I will do it automatically. I am the servant of all great people. Alas, I am the servant of all failures as well. All who are great, I have made great. All who are failures, I have made failures.

I am not a machine; but I work with the precision of a machine and the intellect of a human. Take me, train me, be firm with me, and I'll lay the world at your feet. Be easy with me, and I will destroy you! Who am I? I am your habits!

–Author unknown

nurture physical health

In order to give and foster goodness, you must feel healthy enough to do so. To that end, I cannot stress the significance of caring for your physical health too much. Losing just a small portion of physical health will force you to notice its importance. A sprained back muscle can impair you for weeks at a time. The common cold, a headache, toothache, or slight depression can make you suffer, and long for good health. Small inconveniences like these can make you realize just how much you depend on feeling healthy, while a significant loss of health can really put the value of health into perspective.

When health is lost due to something beyond your control, such as an accident or illness, life can become difficult and painful. However, it is doubly disheartening and frustrating to lose health because of your actions. While you may not be able to stop accidents from happening or change physical conditions that afflict you, be responsible for what is in your control—the way you treat your physical body.

Learn to maintain good habits in order to have the best physical health possible. Good habits encompass a wide variety of factors—eating properly, exercising, getting enough sleep, and caring for your physical condition all play a vital role. When you exercise, your brain releases endorphins that make you feel good naturally, because we are designed to be physically active—the body is healthier because of it. Natural, healthy foods are perfectly designed to fill you with just the right amounts of energy and nutrients, allowing your body to work to its full potential. Be conscious of food choices, levels of exercise, and medical conditions by incorporating healthy habits into your daily life.

While you work to improve health by living a wholesome, well-rounded lifestyle, strive also to remove habits that have detrimental effects. Physical well-being is negatively affected by a lack of exercise, excessive drinking, excessive eating, smoking, lack of sleep, too much stress, and by using drugs of all kinds. You may choose to participate in such activities, but negative habits ultimately work against you. If you overeat, drink excessively, or do not exercise, your body will let you know it is being neglected. You may feel sick, sluggish, tired, and unmotivated. Your mental ability to focus and feel happy will be diminished. Poor physical health causes low self-esteem, irritability, and other negative feelings that work in concert to hinder the body's natural processes and ability to heal. Long-term abuses of your body can be very costly and eventually will catch up with you.

When you need to improve your physical condition, find a way to put that change into motion. You may be able to correct your problems alone, or perhaps will need outside assistance, but the key to success is you. *You* must desire change. Consider a wide range of issues when assessing and correcting bad physical habits. Losing weight and exercising more often, quitting smoking or drinking, and reducing stress while becoming proactive with medical care are just a few of the things you can do. An entire assortment of books, seminars, medical facilities, and various programs can help you achieve and maintain physical health. Loved ones and friends can also offer help and support in your efforts. All of the information and infrastructure is in place, just waiting for you to put it into action.

nurture emotional health

Emotions play a vital role in life; they allow you to process situations and events you encounter and help you cope and come to terms with what you experience, both good and bad. Failing to control or direct your emotions properly can create undesirable thoughts and behaviors that can lead to poor health. Emotions can easily overcome rational, logical thoughts and actions. For instance, if you are angry or sad, those emotions can cause you to do or say things you normally would not. Negative emotions misdirect your focus and take away from your ability to foster goodness. When emotions are uncontrolled, you may act in ways you come to regret. Learn how to deal with emotions effectively and try not to let them overwhelm your rationale and positive perspective.

When you are happy and healthy, you can persuasively encourage and uplift others. If you are depressed or not thinking in a positive state of mind, it will be difficult enough for you to regain a positive, thankful outlook, let alone to pass those views onto others. I've had personal battles with depression and know firsthand of the devastating effects it can have on your life as well as how it affects those closest to you.

Even though life can be challenging, you are ultimately in control of your emotional health; however, if you find that you need help, discover ways to address that challenge—you do not have to fix it alone, help is available. One important point to remember is that a fine line separates emotional health from mental health. If you know of someone who may need help, go to him or her with encouragement and understanding and find a way to offer assistance.

Emotional well-being brings positive feelings of thankfulness, happiness, care, and love. These feelings allow you to focus on life in beneficial ways, helping you promote goodness. Do your best to maintain a positive attitude of gratitude in everything you do, because that is really the core of achieving and maintaining great emotional health.

nurture financial health

When finances are out of order, nearly every aspect of health can be negatively affected, causing physical symptoms of stress ranging from anxiety to nervousness to trouble sleeping. You may feel enormous pressure on your shoulders from financial worry.

Often, financial troubles are of our own making, so we make a complicated situation worse by adding a sense of guilt and despair.

There is always a way out of the stranglehold of financial trouble. In order to find your way back to good financial health, honestly address your situation. The first step is to make wise choices when spending and purchasing. If you have problems with debt, seek advice and information. Do not be ashamed if your financial house is not in order. There is always light at the end of the tunnel—but first you must enter the tunnel. The only way to do that is to take control of your financial position.

You can seek guidance from family, friends, any number of books on the topic, or by legal means. Remember, a bad financial position is not the end of the line, but an opportunity to fix up, renovate, and start anew. Once you begin, you will dramatically lighten the burden you carry and ease the amount of stress you feel.

nurture the health of your conscience

There is no witness so terrible, no accuser so
powerful as conscience which dwells within us.

–Sophocles

A conscience that is not clear leads to a mind that is not clear. When your conscience bothers you, it negatively affects every aspect of life. The energy that could be used to do something positive for yourself and others is wasted on feelings of guilt, sadness, anger, or anxiousness. If you fail to clear your conscience, you are forced to carry a heavy burden, ultimately affecting your mind, spirit, and overall health.

Do you suffer from conscience pests? Conscience pests are those thoughts that creep from your conscience into your mind, where they nag at you. They detract from your well-being by ruining concentration and focus. These pests can literally tear you apart from the inside out.

Here are some possible conscience pests:
- Have you ever hurt or angered someone and know you should apologize, but have not?
- Do you feel worried or stressed when you promise to do something, but consistently put it off?
- Does a person deserve your forgiveness, yet you are not able to offer it?
- Should you say thanks to someone who has helped you in some way?
- Do you want to contact a friend or family member with whom you have lost touch, yet have not done so?
- Have you been selfish and resistant to change—even though your conscience is telling you differently?
- Have you committed hurtful, selfish, or destructive actions?

If you have to spend time and energy repeatedly wrestling to bury conscience pests back into your mind, work to clear them out by taking action to resolve the issues once and for all. Once the negativity is out of the way, the path is clear for you to redirect that energy into more positive thoughts, attitudes, and actions. You may muffle conscience pests for years, but you will not be able to ignore them forever.

Distractions from your conscience make you lose focus on your ability to think and act with goodness. Let go of pride, anger, and guilt by working to clear those pests out of your mind. Identify what you need to fix and take it upon yourself to make it right. Do not wait until it is too late. Clear your conscience now, because in an instant you can lose your opportunity to make amends forever. The everyday pressures of life give you more than enough to worry about, and you should not have to deal with self-inflicted, preventable stress or ill feelings. Let your conscience be your guide and heed the messages it gives you because it is designed to let you know what is right.

When your intelligence don't tell you something ain't right, your conscience gives you a tap on the shoulder and says hold on.

–Elvis Presley

<u>My conscience pests:</u>

1. _____
   _____

2. _____
   _____

3. _____
   _____

4. _____
   _____

5. _____
   _____

6. _____
   _____

7. _____
   _____

8. _____
   _____

What I can do to clear my conscience pests:

1. _____
   _____
2. _____
   _____
3. _____
   _____
4. _____
   _____
5. _____
   _____
6. _____
   _____
7. _____
   _____
8. _____
   _____

take care

Good health gives you the ability to foster the most goodness possible. While this chapter does not give specific directions to maintain health, I hope it encourages you to fully realize the importance of your overall health as it relates to your efforts to promote goodness. The ways you choose to care for your health are personal decisions, and the desire and motivation must ultimately come from you. Many effective means are available to assist and guide you if you actively seek good health and commit to maintain it. Remember to be thankful for the health you have, and put it to good use by fostering goodness throughout your life. Take care.

☑ Action List: Take Care

☒ Improve and maintain physical health:

❑ Make healthy choices and incorporate exercise into your daily routine.
❑ Care for medical conditions.
❑ Limit bad influences on the body.
❑ Seek help to maintain your physical health when necessary.

☒ Improve and maintain spiritual health:

❑ Strengthen spiritual health.
❑ Do not harm, hurt, or be intolerant of others.

☒ Improve and maintain emotional health:

❑ Stay positive in your focus on life.
❑ Help others maintain emotional health.

☒ Improve your financial condition:

❑ Make wise financial choices.
❑ If you need assistance, get advice, information, and a helping hand from family, friends, or professionals.

☒ Clear your conscience:

❑ Find and fix things that weigh upon the health of your conscience.
❑ Take action to resolve any issues you are responsible for—before it's too late.

☒ Improve health to the best of your ability.

☒ Use your health to foster goodness.

My Goals for Better Health

❑ **Physical:** _____

_____

_____

_____

❑ **Emotional:** _____

_____

_____

_____

❑ **Financial:** _____

_____

_____

_____

❑ **Conscience Pests:** _____

_____

_____

_____

_____

9

living on purpose

Life's most urgent question is:
What are you doing for others?

–Dr. Martin Luther King, Jr.

Whether we know it or not, we instinctively search for meaning. The way to fulfill this need is universally similar for every person, yet at the same time, every individual must do so in a unique way. Different aspects of life must be satisfied to find and fulfill your complete purpose. For instance, having faith is not enough if you only care for your needs. Being thankful without being selfless is not enough. Being selfless without a connection to goodness is not enough. Caring for your needs exclusively is not enough. Achieving balance between your needs and selfless responsibilities can help you find complete purpose.

When you are able to manage your needs and concerns, engage in successful relationships, reach your goals and enjoy life, you may be fulfilling certain areas of your life's purpose. However, those areas alone are not enough to find complete meaning. Making an honest effort to connect and live with goodness, maintaining a thankful perspective, and giving selflessly to others can bring deeper meaning and fulfillment to your life.

In order to survive and care for yourself, your loved ones, and your future, it is necessary to engage in a lifestyle you can directly benefit from. That is simply reality. Your goals may include achieving a satisfying lifestyle and caring for you and yours. The desire to feel secure earning your living, anticipating a bright future, and caring for your needs is normal, natural, and necessary, but these things alone will not allow you to find complete meaning; *you have a greater purpose for life.*

You can certainly feel good when achieving goals and dreams, but if they are only associated with material possessions, accomplishments, titles, and center around you alone, you will ultimately learn that those things mean very little in the end. When you only accomplish materialistic and self-serving goals, you may be satisfied for a period of time, but something will always be missing, and no matter how much you cram into your life, a void will remain. One way to fill this emptiness is by living with goodness and selflessness.

Why be good?

Fostering goodness is truly important, and doing so completes a major portion of the puzzle of life's purpose. Learn to let your selfless instincts guide your actions. When you reach the end of life, the legacy that remains is in how selflessly you lived, and what you have done for others. Your thoughts and actions of goodness are what ultimately matter. A profound quote speaks to this issue:

You will find, as you look back upon your life, the moments
that stand out are the moments when you have done things for others.

–Henry Drummond

Why am I here? What's this life for? Have you asked yourself these questions? Maybe you think, "I want to succeed. I want a house and family. I want to make it to the top. I just want to live *my* life." However, do you ever think about what will flash before your eyes as you exhale your last breath of air?

When you draw your last breath, what will you be thinking?
- **You probably won't be thinking about:**
- Material possessions;
- Accomplishments, titles, or positions you have achieved;
- How much money is in the bank;
- Whether or not you had the nicest home;
- Your status or position in life.

- **You may be thinking strongly about:**
- Your connection to Goodness / Faith (or lack thereof);
- How you have (or have not) helped others during your life;
- How you have (or have not) been selfless and good to yourself and others;
- Whether or not you were tolerant and giving.

In my humble opinion, your selfless thoughts and actions, no matter how big or small, are some of the things you will *take with you.* It is easy to be skeptical about my claim since there is no scientific proof to support it. I can offer no measurable data on the subject, nor can I prove it with numeric values or equations. However, it seems to always become clear to people who have been granted a second chance at life following a brush with death. They often make giving and promoting goodness top priorities when living their second chance. Most people do not get a second chance, so it's vitally important to recognize the need to live with goodness before it's too late.

I'm reminded here of a line from one of my favorite movies, <u>Meet Joe Black</u>. The premise of the movie centers on a man, Bill Parrish whose life is at its end. Death has come for him but decides to take human form in order to learn more about life on Earth. Death wants Bill to be its guide because of the fine, upstanding life he led. When Bill's time finally comes for him to move onto that next place, he asks death a question, "Should I be afraid?" Death responds, "Not a man like you." I hope we all live in ways that would allow us to receive an answer like that, if we ever have to ask that question.

Live your life so that the fear of death can never enter your heart.
When you arise in the morning, give thanks for the morning
light. Give thanks for your life and strength. Give thanks for
your food and for the joy of living. And if perchance you see no
reason for giving thanks, rest assured the fault is in yourself.

-Chief Tecumseh, Shawnee Indian Chief

realize

Do not deprive yourself of the things you need to build a safe, secure, and enjoyable environment for you and your loved ones, but remember to think about your responsibility for goodness. Being able to look back on life knowing you have given genuinely and wholeheartedly is a great feeling—a feeling greater than can completely be understood now.

Recognize your blessings and allow selfless instincts to accomplish what they are designed to do. Care for nature. Offer some of your health, time, and money by giving them to others in some way. Learn to truly share. Strive to be generous, kind, trusting, and selfless as much as you possibly can. Have faith and connect to goodness while being tolerant of the ways others do so. Be thankful for all that is in your life, become selfless, take care, and learn to give. Finally, treat others with the "Golden Rule" and find *your* purpose.

☑ Action List: Finding Purpose

☒ Define complete purpose for life:
❏ Reflect on what complete purpose means for you.
❏ Identify and fulfill your needs.
❏ Incorporate goodness into your life to find meaning.

☒ Understand that there is more than a material aspect to life:
❏ Remember, you won't be worrying about material possessions or accomplishments on your deathbed.

☒ Live with goodness by being selfless:
❏ Selfless thoughts and actions, no matter how big or small, are what you will take with you.

☒ Help fulfill your complete purpose by getting back to good:
❏ Have faith.
❏ Connect to goodness.
❏ Be tolerant of the ways in which other people connect.
❏ Be thankful.
❏ Be selfless.
❏ Learn to give.
❏ Take care.
❏ Treat others as you want to be treated.
❏ Be Good.

my purpose is:

Date: _____

_____

_____

_____

_____

_____

_____

_____

_____

_____

_____

People who count on me:

_____

_____

_____

_____

_____

_____

10

on the way...

*You must be the change
you wish to see in the world.*

–Gandhi

All of us are capable of bringing more goodness into the world by caring for ourselves, others, our environment, and living with more tolerance and kindness. We each have something good to give, whether materially or by giving a great, positive attitude. No matter what your goodness is, find a way to give some of it to others. Do it now, while you can.

When you give to someone out of the desire to give, rather than from the need to receive, you have learned to give genuinely. Make a choice to extend goodness to others by being selfless and giving as much as possible. You may not need as much as you think you need and may not want as much as you think you want. This life is a maze you are responsible for navigating, and the only way to reach the true end is to make choices of goodness. Be mindful of your actions, because your actions toward others return twice to you.

Simplicity is pure; simplicity is often truth. As complex and awe-inspiring as nature is, I believe we ultimately exist for simple reasons: to have faith, tend to our lives graciously and respectfully, care for nature, and to be good to one another. Fostering goodness is a major purpose and responsibility for life. Unfortunately, this truth can be easily ignored because no one can force a person to act upon it. You can exist (sometimes quite well in a material sense) by taking care of you and yours exclusively, because living selfishly is an option you have.

Living with goodness is a choice—if you feel it does not matter or is unimportant, you may change your mind when drawing your last breath. Strive to be kind, generous, caring, and helpful to others to the best of your ability. The fact that you are trying to live with goodness will earn rewards for you and the lives you touch.

Realize that you are equal to everyone. When you truly understand and sincerely acknowledge we are one and the same, you will treat others the way they deserve to be treated—with selflessness, dignity, tolerance, respect, compassion, and kindness. You may be more successful, have more money, or be smarter than others, but in the overall picture of life those things make no difference, as everyone has the same ability to offer help, teach, and learn from others in unique ways.

Once again, live your life, take care of yourself and your loved ones, take time for yourself when you need to, and when you are able, give, give, and then give some more...in any way, to any capacity—time, help, and money; tolerance and patience; and top it off by being kind. Give by not gossiping or criticizing, and by truly listening to what others have to say. Share your blessings.

on my way

The way you start your goodness campaign does not make a difference; the most important thing is to start. You do not have to achieve prominence or be written about in history books to reach fantastic goals of goodness, because every act of kindness, helpfulness, or patience is extremely important and equally powerful in the big picture.

Goodness affects everything in exponential ways. If you do one good thing, even something as simple as driving courteously, saying thank you, or offering material help to someone in need, you are doing good. In turn, this leads to more acts of goodness, such as repairing relationships or giving kindness, love, patience, forgiveness, and tolerance. Every good action is important, and the world will be that much better for it.

Set an example by living with goodness, but always allow others the freedom to find their own path, because it means different things to different people. There are religious, cultural, social, and personal differences that are good in their own way, and each can serve in some capacity to help bring humanity back to good.

Negativity will continue even when you foster goodness, but do not let that fact hinder your efforts. Of course, there will be occasions when you are treated badly, as you may experience selfishness, intolerance, or cruelty. This is an unfortunate certainty. However, do not use it as an excuse to extend bad behaviors or thoughts toward others. Live with goodness because it is the right thing to do—not because you expect it in return.

Do not let the actions of others deter or detour your actions of goodness by finding effective ways to deal with negativity. Realize when you are able to deal with negative circumstances, situations, and people, and learn to know when you must remove yourself from a situation before it causes you to think and act negatively.

You can make the world a better place by remaining true to goodness to the best of your ability. Of course, there will be times when you fall short and get discouraged by what you or others do, say, or think, so don't be too tough on yourself if you lose your way. Instead, work to find your way back to good.

*The first great gift we can
bestow on others is a good example.*

-Thomas Morell

As I said before, you may not be able to end world hunger or bring world peace, but through your thoughts and actions of goodness, you will do your part to bring our world back to good, especially when you recognize opportunities in your life and act on them. Teach *and* learn about goodness from those around you; from spiritual beliefs, from your family and friends, from children, and from others you encounter. Commit to live with goodness in every aspect of life.

Participating in your campaign will allow goodness to flow through you into our world. From our differences to our fundamental similarities; from our unique, personal views and beliefs to the elements we share on a universal level, we are one and the same—bound to goodness and life together. Now is the time for you to make a difference in your life, which in turn makes a difference for humanity and our world.

What difference have you made in the world by living with goodness? The answer may be short or may branch out and touch many lives. Only you can write your answer. No one can force you to exhibit true, selfless goodness; but ultimately, you are responsible and accountable for your actions. Each day you're alive, you are impacting the lives of others; if your life has not fostered goodness in one form or another, then you have lived for nothing. Do you want to take that to the grave?

Do all the good you can,
By all the means you can,
In all the ways you can,
In all the places you can,
To all the people you can,
As long as ever you can.

–John Wesley

**Following is your 30–Day inspirational Journal.
Enjoy and make your difference!**

30-day Goodness Campaign - Day 1

Date: _____

❑ **Good For Others: Family / Friends / Nature / Others:**

_____

_____

_____

_____

_____

_____

❑ **Good for Myself: Mind / Body / Spirit / Financial / Other:**

_____

_____

_____

_____

_____

_____

❑ **Today, I am grateful for & noticed ...**

_____

_____

_____

_____

_____

_____

We must not, in trying to think about how we can make a big difference, ignore the small daily differences we can make, which, over time, add up to big differences that we often cannot foresee.

–Marian Wright Edelman

30 – day Goodness Campaign - Day 2

Date: _____

❑ **Good For Others: Family / Friends / Nature / Others:**

_____

_____

_____

_____

_____

_____

_____

❑ **Good for Myself: Mind / Body / Spirit / Financial / Other:**

_____

_____

_____

_____

_____

_____

_____

❑ **Today, I am grateful for & noticed ...**

_____

_____

_____

_____

_____

_____

Unless we think of others and do something for
them, we miss one of the greatest sources of happiness.

–Ray Lyman Wilbur

30 – day Goodness Campaign - Day 3

Date: _____

❑ Good For Others: Family / Friends / Nature / Others:

_____

_____

_____

_____

_____

_____

❑ Good for Myself: Mind / Body / Spirit / Financial / Other:

_____

_____

_____

_____

_____

_____

❑ Today, I am grateful for & noticed ...

_____

_____

_____

_____

_____

_____

The Optimist Creed

Promise Yourself...

To be so strong that nothing
can disturb your peace of mind.

To talk health, happiness and
prosperity to every person you meet.

To make all your friends
feel that there is something in them.

To look at the sunny side of
everything and make your optimism come true.

To think only of the best, to work only
for the best, and to expect only the best.

To be just as enthusiastic about the
success of others as you are about your own.

To forget the mistakes of the past and
press on to the greater achievements of the future.

To wear a cheerful countenance at all times
and give every living creature you meet a smile.

To give so much time to the improvement
of yourself that you have no time to criticize others.

To be too large for worry, too noble for anger,
too strong for fear, and too happy to permit the presence of trouble.

-Christian D. Larson

30 – day Goodness Campaign - Day 4

Date: _____

❑ **Good For Others: Family / Friends / Nature / Others:**

_____

_____

_____

_____

_____

_____

_____

❑ **Good for Myself: Mind / Body / Spirit / Financial / Other:**

_____

_____

_____

_____

_____

_____

_____

❑ **Today, I am grateful for & noticed …**

_____

_____

_____

_____

_____

_____

_____

*Real integrity is doing the right thing, knowing
that nobody's going to know whether you did it or not.*

–Oprah Winfrey

30 – day Goodness Campaign - Day 5

Date: _____

❑ **Good For Others: Family / Friends / Nature / Others:**

_____

_____

_____

_____

_____

_____

_____

❑ **Good for Myself: Mind / Body / Spirit / Financial / Other:**

_____

_____

_____

_____

_____

_____

_____

❑ **Today, I am grateful for & noticed …**

_____

_____

_____

_____

_____

_____

_____

The Critic

It is not the critic who counts, nor the man who points out how the strong man stumbled or where the doer of deeds could have done them better. The credit belongs to the man who is actually in the arena, whose face is marred by dust and sweat and blood; who strives valiantly, who errs and comes short again and again, who knows the great enthusiasm, the great devotions, and spends himself in a worthy cause; who at the best knows in the end the triumph of high achievement, and who at the worst, if he fails, at least fails while daring greatly so that his place shall never be with those cold and timid souls who know neither victory nor defeat.

–President Theodore Roosevelt

30 – day Goodness Campaign - Day 6

Date: _____

❑ **Good For Others: Family / Friends / Nature / Others:**

_____

_____

_____

_____

_____

_____

❑ **Good for Myself: Mind / Body / Spirit / Financial / Other:**

_____

_____

_____

_____

_____

❑ **Today, I am grateful for & noticed ...**

_____

_____

_____

_____

_____

Hungry not only for bread—but hungry for love. Naked not only for clothing—but naked for human dignity and respect. Homeless not only for want of a room of bricks—but homeless because of rejection.

–Mother Teresa

30 – day Goodness Campaign - Day 7

Date: _____

❑ **Good For Others: Family / Friends / Nature / Others:**

_____

_____

_____

_____

_____

_____

❑ **Good for Myself: Mind / Body / Spirit / Financial / Other:**

_____

_____

_____

_____

_____

_____

❑ **Today, I am grateful for & noticed ...**

_____

_____

_____

_____

_____

_____

If you have much, give of your wealth;
if you have little, give of your heart.

–Arabian Proverb

30 – day Goodness Campaign - Day 8

Date: _____

❑ Good For Others: Family / Friends / Nature / Others:

_____

_____

_____

_____

_____

_____

_____

❑ Good for Myself: Mind / Body / Spirit / Financial / Other:

_____

_____

_____

_____

_____

_____

_____

❑ Today, I am grateful for & noticed ...

_____

_____

_____

_____

_____

_____

If I have been of service; if I have glimpsed more of the nature and essence of ultimate good; if I am inspired to reach wider horizons of thought and action; if I am at peace with myself; it has been a successful day.

–Alex Nobel

30 – day Goodness Campaign - Day 9

Date: _____

❏ Good For Others: Family / Friends / Nature / Others:

_____

_____

_____

_____

_____

_____

❏ Good for Myself: Mind / Body / Spirit / Financial / Other:

_____

_____

_____

_____

_____

❏ Today, I am grateful for & noticed …

_____

_____

_____

_____

_____

_____

*Not he who has much is
rich, but he who gives much.*

–Erich Fromm

30 – day Goodness Campaign - Day 10

Date: _____

❑ **Good For Others: Family / Friends / Nature / Others:**

_____

_____

_____

_____

_____

_____

❑ **Good for Myself: Mind / Body / Spirit / Financial / Other:**

_____

_____

_____

_____

_____

_____

❑ **Today, I am grateful for & noticed …**

_____

_____

_____

_____

_____

I have one life and one chance to make it count for something…I'm free to choose what that something is, and the something I've chosen is my faith. Now my faith goes beyond theology and religion and requires considerable work and effort. My faith demands—this is not optional—my faith demands that I do whatever I can, wherever I am, whenever I can, for as long as I can, with whatever I have, to try to make a difference.

–Jimmy Carter

30 – day Goodness Campaign - Day 11

Date: _____

❑ Good For Others: Family / Friends / Nature / Others:

_____

_____

_____

_____

_____

_____

❑ Good for Myself: Mind / Body / Spirit / Financial / Other:

_____

_____

_____

_____

_____

_____

❑ Today, I am grateful for & noticed …

_____

_____

_____

_____

_____

_____

Keep your dreams alive. Understand to achieve anything requires faith and belief in yourself, vision, hard work, determination, and dedication. Remember all things are possible for those who believe.

–Gail Devers

30 – day Goodness Campaign - Day 12

Date: _____

❑ **Good For Others: Family / Friends / Nature / Others:**

_____

_____

_____

_____

_____

_____

_____

❑ **Good for Myself: Mind / Body / Spirit / Financial / Other:**

_____

_____

_____

_____

_____

_____

❑ **Today, I am grateful for & noticed ...**

_____

_____

_____

_____

_____

_____

*The world is more malleable than you think
and it's waiting for you to hammer it into shape.*

—Bono

30 – day Goodness Campaign - Day 13

Date: _____

❑ Good For Others: Family / Friends / Nature / Others:

_____

_____

_____

_____

_____

_____

❑ Good for Myself: Mind / Body / Spirit / Financial / Other:

_____

_____

_____

_____

_____

_____

❑ Today, I am grateful for & noticed ...

_____

_____

_____

_____

_____

_____

Be happy. Talk happiness. Happiness calls out responsive gladness in others. There is enough sadness in the world without yours.... never doubt the excellence and permanence of what is yet to be. Join the great company of those who make the barren places of life fruitful with kindness.... Your success and happiness lie in you.... The great enduring realities are love and service.... Resolve to keep happy and your joy and you shall form an invincible host against difficulties.

— **Helen Keller**

30 – day Goodness Campaign - Day 14

Date: _____

❑ Good For Others: Family / Friends / Nature / Others:

_____

_____

_____

_____

_____

_____

❑ Good for Myself: Mind / Body / Spirit / Financial / Other:

_____

_____

_____

_____

_____

❑ Today, I am grateful for & noticed …

_____

_____

_____

_____

_____

5 Keys to Happiness:

1. Free your heart from hatred
2. Free your mind from worries
3. Live simple
4. Give more
5. Expect less

—Unknown

30 – day Goodness Campaign - Day 15

Date: _____

❑ Good For Others: Family / Friends / Nature / Others:

_____

_____

_____

_____

_____

_____

❑ Good for Myself: Mind / Body / Spirit / Financial / Other:

_____

_____

_____

_____

_____

_____

❑ Today, I am grateful for & noticed …

_____

_____

_____

_____

_____

_____

*To work for the common
good is the greatest creed.*

–Woodrow Wilson

30 – day Goodness Campaign - Day 16

Date: _____

❑ **Good For Others: Family / Friends / Nature / Others:**

_____

_____

_____

_____

_____

_____

_____

❑ **Good for Myself: Mind / Body / Spirit / Financial / Other:**

_____

_____

_____

_____

_____

_____

❑ **Today, I am grateful for & noticed ...**

_____

_____

_____

_____

_____

_____

Everyone who is seriously interested in the pursuit of science becomes convinced that a spirit is manifest in the laws of the universe—a spirit vastly superior to man, and one in the face of which our modest powers must feel humble.

–Albert Einstein

30 – day Goodness Campaign - Day 17

Date: _____

❑ Good For Others: Family / Friends / Nature / Others:

_____

_____

_____

_____

_____

_____

❑ Good for Myself: Mind / Body / Spirit / Financial / Other:

_____

_____

_____

_____

_____

_____

❑ Today, I am grateful for & noticed …

_____

_____

_____

_____

_____

_____

As much as we need a prosperous economy,
we also need a prosperity of kindness and decency.

-Caroline Kennedy

30 – day Goodness Campaign - Day 18

Date:

❑ Good For Others: Family / Friends / Nature / Others:

_____

_____

_____

_____

_____

_____

❑ Good for Myself: Mind / Body / Spirit / Financial / Other:

_____

_____

_____

_____

_____

_____

❑ Today, I am grateful for & noticed …

_____

_____

_____

_____

_____

_____

How lovely to think that no one need wait a moment, we can start now, start slowly changing the world. How lovely that everyone, great and small, can make their contribution…how we can always, always give something, if only kindness.

–Anne Frank

30 – day Goodness Campaign - Day 19

Date: _____

❑ **Good For Others: Family / Friends / Nature / Others:**

_____

_____

_____

_____

_____

_____

_____

❑ **Good for Myself: Mind / Body / Spirit / Financial / Other:**

_____

_____

_____

_____

_____

_____

_____

❑ **Today, I am grateful for & noticed …**

_____

_____

_____

_____

_____

_____

_____

I have found that among its other
benefits, giving liberates the soul of the giver.

-Maya Angelou

30 – day Goodness Campaign - Day 20

Date:

❑ **Good For Others: Family / Friends / Nature / Others:**

_____

_____

_____

_____

_____

_____

_____

❑ **Good for Myself: Mind / Body / Spirit / Financial / Other:**

_____

_____

_____

_____

_____

_____

❑ **Today, I am grateful for & noticed …**

_____

_____

_____

_____

_____

_____

Try not to become a man of success,
but rather try to become a man of value.

-Albert Einstein

30 – day Goodness Campaign - Day 21

Date: _____

❑ Good For Others: Family / Friends / Nature / Others:

_____

_____

_____

_____

_____

_____

❑ Good for Myself: Mind / Body / Spirit / Financial / Other:

_____

_____

_____

_____

_____

_____

❑ Today, I am grateful for & noticed …

_____

_____

_____

_____

_____

_____

That best portion of a good man's life, his little,
nameless, unremembered acts of kindness and of love.

*- **William Wordsworth***

30 – day Goodness Campaign - Day 22

Date: _____

❑ **Good For Others: Family / Friends / Nature / Others:**

_____

_____

_____

_____

_____

_____

❑ **Good for Myself: Mind / Body / Spirit / Financial / Other:**

_____

_____

_____

_____

_____

❑ **Today, I am grateful for & noticed …**

_____

_____

_____

_____

_____

*Faith is the strength by which
a shattered world will emerge into the light.*

–Helen Keller

30 – day Goodness Campaign - Day 23

<u>**Date:**</u> _____

❑ <u>**Good For Others: Family / Friends / Nature / Others:**</u>

_____

_____

_____

_____

_____

_____

❑ <u>**Good for Myself: Mind / Body / Spirit / Financial / Other:**</u>

_____

_____

_____

_____

_____

_____

❑ <u>**Today, I am grateful for & noticed …**</u>

_____

_____

_____

_____

_____

_____

The world is my country,
and my religion is to do good.

-Thomas Paine

30 – day Goodness Campaign - Day 24

Date: _____

❑ **Good For Others: Family / Friends / Nature / Others:**

_____

_____

_____

_____

_____

_____

❑ **Good for Myself: Mind / Body / Spirit / Financial / Other:**

_____

_____

_____

_____

_____

❑ **Today, I am grateful for & noticed …**

_____

_____

_____

_____

_____

_____

As long as I can conceive something better than myself,
I cannot be easy unless I am striving to bring it into existence.

–George Bernard Shaw

30 – day Goodness Campaign - Day 25

Date: _____

❑ Good For Others: Family / Friends / Nature / Others:

_____

_____

_____

_____

_____

❑ Good for Myself: Mind / Body / Spirit / Financial / Other:

_____

_____

_____

_____

_____

❑ Today, I am grateful for & noticed ...

_____

_____

_____

_____

_____

_____

<u>Day Dream</u>

Dawn starts to break and birds begin nature's morning revelry.
The sun softly begins its workday, illuminating the landscape. Edging over
the eastern horizon, a yellow-orange glow appears
and nature awakens to its full glory.

Midday sun brightly lights the bright, blue sky,
contrasted by puffy white clouds.
By noon, the sun is blazing in full glory, heating and feeding our planet.

Evening time. The day starts its daily surrender to
dusk…and then to night. The sun, seemingly weary and tired,
swells and relaxes into its familiar orange hue,
slowly sinking into the western horizon.

Did you take a moment and notice all the beauty of nature around you today?
-ken ferrara

30 – day Goodness Campaign - Day 26

Date: _____

❏ **Good For Others: Family / Friends / Nature / Others:**

_____

_____

_____

_____

_____

_____

❏ **Good for Myself: Mind / Body / Spirit / Financial / Other:**

_____

_____

_____

_____

_____

❏ **Today, I am grateful for & noticed ...**

_____

_____

_____

_____

_____

Carry out a random act of kindness,
with no expectation of reward, safe in the
knowledge that one day someone might do the same for you.

-Princess Diana

30 – day Goodness Campaign - Day 27

Date: _____

❑ **Good For Others: Family / Friends / Nature / Others:**

_____

_____

_____

_____

_____

_____

❑ **Good for Myself: Mind / Body / Spirit / Financial / Other:**

_____

_____

_____

_____

_____

_____

❑ **Today, I am grateful for & noticed …**

_____

_____

_____

_____

_____

_____

*Kindness is the language which
the deaf can hear and the blind can see.*

-Mark Twain

30 – day Goodness Campaign - Day 28

Date:

❑ Good For Others: Family / Friends / Nature / Others:

_____

_____

_____

_____

_____

_____

_____

❑ Good for Myself: Mind / Body / Spirit / Financial / Other:

_____

_____

_____

_____

_____

_____

_____

❑ Today, I am grateful for & noticed …

_____

_____

_____

_____

_____

_____

_____

And as I've gotten older, I've had more of
a tendency to look for people who live by kindness,
tolerance, compassion, a gentler way of looking at things.

-Martin Scorsese

30 – day Goodness Campaign - Day 29

Date: _____

❑ **Good For Others: Family / Friends / Nature / Others:**

_____

_____

_____

_____

_____

_____

❑ **Good for Myself: Mind / Body / Spirit / Financial / Other:**

_____

_____

_____

_____

_____

_____

❑ **Today, I am grateful for & noticed ...**

_____

_____

_____

_____

_____

_____

*Goodness is the only
investment that never fails.*

-Henry David Thoreau

30 – day Goodness Campaign - Day 30

Date:

❏ **Good For Others: Family / Friends / Nature / Others:**

_____

_____

_____

_____

_____

_____

❏ **Good for Myself: Mind / Body / Spirit / Financial / Other:**

_____

_____

_____

_____

_____

❏ **Today, I am grateful for & noticed ...**

_____

_____

_____

_____

_____

from the author

I wanted to change the world,
but I found that the only thing one
can be sure of changing is oneself.

–Aldous Huxley

I like to quote the statement above when people ask me what inspired me to write this book. I was tired of the negativity and pessimism in my life as well as in the world at large. I was mean, impatient, intolerant, and noticed the constant violence, greed and selfishness everywhere I looked. I would make comments and observations in the background, armchair quarterbacking people I knew and society in general. This lead me to ask, "Why can't people show more kindness and be more giving, trusting, grateful, and understanding? Why do people have to be selfish and negative?" Of course, in my mind, it was always 'people,' that were the cause…never me doing any of the damage.

I remember thinking about my life and the state of our world—how troubled it seemed at times, and honestly felt I did my fair share to help. You know what? I did do my fair share—of negativity and pessimism. It wasn't until years of separation from my family and many talks with my grandma that I slowly became aware of the fact that the responsibility for much of the negativity I witnessed in the world, at work, and in my family was my own. Trapped in a downward spiral, I was often angry, resentful, ungrateful, and selfish.

My motto was, "What's in it for me?" If something did not directly affect or pertain to me, then it was someone else's problem. I was so wrapped up in an "all about me" attitude, that I could not see the ways I

181

perceived and treated others lacked goodness—that I was treating people in the very ways I found so disheartening. The words I, me, my, and mine were used much too often in everyday encounters, and self-centered, intolerant behavior served to drain positive energy and joy from my life. My actions caused personal relationships to suffer, creating damaging rifts in my family, social, and professional lives.

• **Here's a glimpse into what brought me to where I am today.**

"A baby girl!" shouted the Doctor, as he hurriedly passed my little daughter to the nurse, anxiously waiting to perform the routine tests that newborns receive. I looked at my girlfriend, Jen. She was exhausted and pale after thirteen hours of labor but managed to crack a smile. I stroked her hair and gave her a kiss on the cheek. "We did it, babe," I whispered, trying to show more confidence than I was feeling. We were young, scared, and excited at the same time.

The year was 1994. We had been dating for just over 5 years, but now life was forcing some huge, life-changing adjustments—the baby's cries constantly reminded us of that fact. We were relatively young at 21 years old, but decided we were going to make it. I quit my last year of college and took a job with the local phone company, while Jen stayed home with our baby. Thankfully, my parents invited us to live in my old bedroom until we got on our feet, because the $7.43 an hour I was making made money a little tight.

Within a year, we were out in an apartment and doing our best to get by. Daily life encouraged and reminded us to press on, as we tried to remain aware and thankful for our many blessings. As life became busier, time went by and years passed. Before we knew it, our daughter was nearly three years old. Throughout that time, however, things changed between us. There was awkward tension in the air when Jen and I spent time together, and our relationship just didn't feel the same. Maybe it was due to our hectic schedules, me working days and Jen working nights and weekends; or, perhaps that feeling was coming from somewhere deep within myself.

By 1997, I had gotten out of shape and was unhealthy. To be perfectly honest, I focused selfishly myself. By doing so, my outlook on life, my mood, and my abilities were affected negatively. I was always tired and crabby, pushing away those closest to me and causing relationships to strain. Jen and I ended up splitting up for three long years, putting our precious daughter through hell.

Following years of stubborn selfishness, and the pain, self-pity, and unhappiness it produced, I began to ask, "Why am I so mean and negative at times? Why do I consider my needs to be more important than the needs of others? What can I do to bring more happiness and fulfillment into my life? How can I become a better person, both for myself, as well as for the people around me?"

After many heart to hearts with Busia and my family, and enough time alone with my thoughts, I finally woke up to the fact that in order for this world to change, I must be the one to change. Of course, saying I would stop thinking and acting negatively was much easier than doing it. But goodness, in all of its facets and dimensions, brings about such powerfully positive, productive results that I simply had to try my hardest to change for the better—after all, you only get what you give.

From 1997 through 1999, I reached some low and scary points in life. I was separated from the ones I loved, depressed, angry, and even in trouble with the law. At times, I felt like I was out on an island—alone. To borrow from John Donne, I now understand that "no man is an island." Eventually, I overcame much of the negativity and pessimism in my life with faith, help from family and friends, and using some of the age-old ideas in this book. By 2000, Jen and I had reconciled and were married in early 2001.

To be perfectly honest, I still struggle to follow the very advice and instruction on these pages because life can be hard. I have some difficult relationships in my family, and sometimes must work hard to see my life's glass as half full. Choosing to be good is simply tougher than me at times, but I've learned to trust that life is a journey; a daily process with ups and downs, with bright lights and pitch blackness.

Different situations and challenges all serve in some way to help us learn to choose goodness to the best of our ability. Do I falter in this journey called life? Of course. Do I have to remove my shoe from my mouth? From time to time (okay, maybe a little more often than not). Overall, I can genuinely say working to get back to good empowers me to improve my perspective and enriches my relationships, my health, and my heart and soul. I'm sincerely and enthusiastically certain it can do the same for you.

The ideas I've compiled here are the combined result of some of my life experience coupled with the wisdom imparted by those people who consistently embody the best attributes of the human spirit. I have assembled knowledge and lessons learned from personal struggles, hardships, and times of joy, as well as from examples of countless people who have shown the true goodness we are capable of, into something tangible and measurable—something that you can practice on a daily basis to help resolve questions, negativities, and challenges of life.

Participating in the goodness campaign has the potential to make every day a better day. You can fuel your campaign with proper lifestyle changes and by incorporating healthy eating and exercise habits into your everyday routines. (This was a very important step in my journey, which incidentally is one major reason I started writing.) Improving relationships by apologizing to others and forgiving, as well as maintaining a sense of gratitude and having faith are essential to getting back to good.

Of course, as I mentioned earlier, life isn't a fairy tale—hardships and challenges will still exist; but faith, positive focus, and great actions for yourself and others can help you find the goodness and happiness that is available for everyone to enjoy and share. My most sincere hope is to inspire you to focus on the positive and bring balance to your life. By presenting gentle reminders for you to bring more kindness, care, compassion, and gratefulness into your life every day through a little campaign, I hope you will find and enjoy all the truly rich and fulfilling benefits living with goodness brings.

All my best...
ken ferrara, j.r.g (just a regular guy☺)

about the book

I am the first to admit you won't find any astonishing revelations, Earth-shattering insights, or complex philosophies on these pages. Many of the ideas expressed are as old as time, and I do not claim to present any new, fundamental beliefs or ideas that have not been written about, thought of, or discussed before by people much smarter and more insightful than myself. However, the information on these pages, from fundamental concepts to age-old knowledge, ultimately relates to our common link to goodness. The responsibility for living with goodness encompasses and applies to all people equally, no matter race, creed, or country, and is something we can focus on every day, in each of our lives.

You won't find complicated comparisons of differing cultures or religions on these pages, as this book was written to be accessible and beneficial to people of all backgrounds and faiths. I hold extreme reverence for the multitude of differing beliefs in our diverse world because everyone travels a personal journey in life and has unique experiences and perspectives.

My most heartfelt wish is to respect differing views, while offering the positive, powerful, and practical values goodness provides. To that end, I have tried my best to express ideas and messages in ways that do not detract from particular beliefs, encouraging us to live with the goodness and tolerance that is applicable to everyone. Above all, this book's fundamental message of doing something good each day can become an integral part of a person's life regardless of spiritual, social, or personal perspectives and beliefs.

From calling someone you have lost touch with to smiling at the person next to you, to making up with your siblings (I'm trying hard), *every* good thought and action will help bring our world back to good. Life is too short to wait for the next person to do it; take it upon yourself to be that next person—and pass it on.

My Debts of Gratitude

Thank God...

for giving all through many names, forms, words, interpretations, and faces. I understand that each day we see another sunrise is a gift. I am forever thankful for our ability to know, the power to love, the beauty of nature, and for the miracle of life.

To my wife,

Thanks for your constant support and encouragement. Through the years, you helped me keep pen to paper and motivated me even when I pushed away. Thanks for your insight, endless patience in our apartment, and your ability to understand me. I love you.

To my kids,

Thanks for your stern hand in making sure I would finish, and for keeping our secret. You sacrificed many things because Dad was always "working on the book." You waited so patiently through my mood swings and procrastination, and took many, many trips to Great America with Mom until this final copy was ready. Well, here it is G, Bri, and T. Now we can practice hockey, fly kites, and build snowmen. I love you guys.

To my parents,

Thanks for your help over the years and for the countless hours you sat by my side, encouraging me. Although I was often the "Jack" of the family, the lessons I learned helped me understand and know more about myself and grow. In this little paragraph, I cannot begin to express my gratitude, Love, Ken.

To my grandparents,

To Busia, Dziadzio, and Grammy: Thank you so much for your love and generosity. I will always carry your love and patience in my heart. I am forever thankful for what you have given me and for what you continue to teach. I could not have completed this book without your help (especially recently, Busia). Love, Kenosha, Kenoosh. An-i-mal

For the rest of my family & friends,

Mike, Anita, Brandon, Nathan, and Madelyn, Gary, Dawn, Jax, Austyn, and Connyr, Sal, Joyce and family; to Auntie; Jim, Karen and family; Licha and family; To Keith, Alice and Hailey, Bryan, and Samuel, Kissy and Lena, Zack and Sunshine (you inspired me so much when I saw a copy of my first edition on your shelf-thank you); Michelle & family; Mike (Big Stix), Martha and Family; Jimmy, Julie and family, and to the Shea's. To Mrs. Curan and my bud Kurt; thank you all for giving me the insight, knowledge, and encouragement to complete this book. To Renee and Joe, Thanks for helping me with your challenges and examples.

Simple Inspiration

I cannot remember where I read or heard this story, so the credit is not mine. I have simply paraphrased it to the best of my recollection:

There is an old tale about Heaven and hell (use your own words for Good and evil here) that goes a little something like this:

One day, God finally decided to let people know what happens after death. A group of people was selected to visit that 'next place,' and would then come back to Earth to report the findings to the world. The people went on their journey, and, truth be told, there really is a Heaven and a hell.

Heaven, to the surprise of the visitors, is a vast banquet hall, with a table full of the most delicious food and drink ever seen. The table is very wide, and long enough to fit every soul that sits to eat. Everyone in Heaven gets hungry often, and needs to eat several times each day. Luckily, there is always plenty of food and drink. Unfortunately, everyone has arms that are as long as the table is wide, and their arms cannot bend, so they are unable to feed themselves.

Hell has the same configuration—people seated at a wide banquet table with the same unbendable arms. Delicious food graces this table also. The daily hunger for the people in hell is ravenous and painful. Luckily, hell has an abundance of food and drink for everyone, as well.

In Heaven, everyone is able to eat and is cared for, because everybody looks out for the needs of others by extending their arms to feed the person across the table from them, since they cannot feed themselves. With the abundance that exists, no one ever leaves hungry or has to do without.

Down in hell, people are only concerned with trying to feed themselves.

Since their arms do not bend, they cannot feed themselves, so no one eats. They suffer the extreme pain of starvation because they choose not to extend their arms to each other and help one another to eat, so everyone suffers. The abundance of food only serves to enhance their suffering. Even though there is always more than enough food to go around, selfish people only look out for their own needs, and would rather starve then try to help someone else. That is the philosophy of a selfish existence.

Our lives are not very different from that example of Heaven and hell. There is an abundance of good things in life that every person can enjoy, and more than enough to go around, if we learn to perceive positively, truly share, and give to one another.

The bottom line is that we all need help at some point in life, and we are able to help others at different times (or ways) during life. Simplistic? Maybe. However, these facts could not be more true. Everyone has areas in life that need improvement in order to bring us to that end. ***Let's work on this together!***

Definition

getting back to good, *v.n.* **1.** the choice one makes to live with goodness **2.** the process by which a person connects with goodness. **3.** to be tolerant of differing views and beliefs. **4.** to achieve and maintain a perspective of thankfulness for everything in life. **5.** the process by which a person recognizes selfishness and turns it into selflessness. **6.** to give: *help, kindness, tolerance, forgiveness, care for nature, patience, compassion, thankfulness, etc.* **7.** to care for all aspects of health in order to foster goodness to one's full potential. **8.** the process of combining definitions 1–7 to find and fulfill complete purpose for life. **9.** to be good...*and nice* ☒

☑ Action List Summary & Notes
Look Up, Be Thankful

☒ **Be thankful for each new day:**
  ❏ Remember that every day is a gift—for you personally, as well as for the world.

☒ **Are there some tragedies or hardships that you have undergone and become stronger because of them?**
  ❏ Use your experience as a foundation for helping someone else going through challenging situations.

☒ **Be thankful for your health:**
  ❏ Remember that health is ultimately not in your hands.

☒ **Be thankful for your abilities:**
  ❏ Realize your abilities are gifts.
  ❏ Be humble.

☒ **Remove obstacles that hinder a thankful perspective.**

☒ **Stop taking things for granted:**
  ❏ Consciously think about and be grateful for what is in your life.
  ❏ Show gratitude in thought as well as action.
  ❏ Recognize that you are not entitled to health, happiness, or a good life—they are gifts.
  ❏ Be thankful for and humbled by the gifts you receive.

☒ **Be willing to accept that adversity may strike at any time.**

☒ **Be thankful through tough times:**
    ❑ Always find something to be thankful for, no matter what situation you are going through.
    ❑ Find thankful ways to deal with tough situations.

☒ **Do not pity yourself because of circumstances in life:**
    ❑ View life with thankfulness instead of pity.
    ❑ Do not compare your problems with the problems of others.
    ❑ Remember, your situation could always be worse.
    ❑ View adversity as something that will make you stronger.
    ❑ Be happy for others when good fortune embraces them.

☒ **Try not to worry about what cannot be controlled:**
    ❑ Much of life is beyond your control.
    ❑ Do not get so caught up with the details of life that you forget to act with thankfulness and goodness.
    ❑ Convert the energy spent on worrying into thankful thoughts and actions.

☒ **Strengthen your thankful perspective.**

☒ **Fill in your *I am thankful for:* checklist:**
    ❑ Reflect on and write down everything you should be thankful for, from a new day, to health, to the goodness of humanity.

❑ Review your checklist several times a day and add to it often.

❑ Establish a routine for daily gratitude.

☒ Maintain an attitude of gratitude to the best of your ability:

❑ Take heart in the fact that people have gone through terrible situations and have been able to maintain a thankful perspective. So can you!

❑ Share some of the gifts you receive with others.

❑ Remember that a life clouded with selfishness cannot maintain a thankful perspective.

☒ Couple your thankful perspective with thankful actions of goodness.

<u>Notes:</u>

☑ Selfish to Selfless

☒ Learn to identify and shun selfishness:

❏ Identify selfish thoughts and behaviors, large and small.

❏ Do not rationalize that you are not selfish simply because you have not broken any laws or committed significant actions of selfishness.

❏ Recognize that selfishness covers everything from intolerance, to stealing, to making fun of someone, to judging others.

☒ Selfishness can be changed:

❏ Foster goodness by replacing selfishness with selflessness.

☒ Make a personal to-do list to encourage selflessness.

☒ Assess your thoughts and actions:

❏ Get an objective opinion to help you identify your strengths and weaknesses.

❏ List your selfish behaviors, make a plan, and commit to become selfless.

☒ Be selfless to the best of your ability.

☒ Do not judge others with respect to their possessions or lifestyle, as long as no hurt or harm is caused:

❏ Recognize that everyone is accountable for his or her own lifestyle and actions.

Notes:

_____

_____

_____

_____

_____

_____

_____

_____

_____

_____

_____

_____

_____

_____

_____

_____

_____

_____

_____

_____

_____

_____

_____

_____

_____

_____

_____

☑ Giving

☒ Give personal tolerance:
❑ Do your best to tolerate unique viewpoints, lifestyles, and physical characteristics, as long as they do not cause hate or harm.
❑ Be as tolerant of the shortcomings of others as you are of your own.
❑ Do not force your views or opinions on others.

☒ Give spiritual tolerance:
❑ Do not force your spiritual views upon others.
❑ Practice tolerance by remembering your spiritual preference is not necessarily correct for everyone.

☒ Give help to others:
❑ Offering help is one of the best things you can do in life.
❑ Offer help in many different and unique ways.
❑ Do not miss an opportunity to help someone—you will need help someday.

☒ Give forgiveness to others:
❑ Replace feelings of hurt and anger by forgiving.
❑ Forgive as a means to release grudges that take away from your ability to foster goodness.
❑ Give Type II forgiveness to help you offer Type I Forgiveness.

☒ Give Kindness to others:
❑ Allow the natural trait of kindness to surface in your daily life.
❑ Every kind action is grand because of its potential for goodness.
❑ Give with kindness.

☒ **Give Environmentally:**
- ❑ Do not waste precious natural resources.
- ❑ Find ways to help our environment.

☒ **Create your own To-Do list—Giving.**

☒ **Remember, *giving* is good:**
- ❑ Giving fulfills you in fundamental ways that simply are not reachable by any other means.

Notes:

_____

_____

_____

_____

_____

_____

_____

_____

_____

_____

_____

_____

_____

_____

_____

_____

_____

_____

_____

_____

_____

_____

_____

_____

_____

☑ Take Care

⊠ Improve and maintain physical health:

❑ Make healthy choices and incorporate exercise into your daily routine.
❑ Care for medical conditions.
❑ Limit bad influences on the body.
❑ Seek help to maintain your physical health when necessary.

⊠ Improve and maintain spiritual health:

❑ Strengthen spiritual health.
❑ Do not harm, hurt, or be intolerant of others.

⊠ Improve and maintain emotional health:

❑ Stay positive in your focus on life.
❑ Help others maintain emotional health.

⊠ Improve your financial condition:

❑ Make wise financial choices.
❑ If you need assistance, get advice, information, and a helping hand from family, friends, or professionals.

⊠ Clear your conscience:

❑ Find and fix things that weigh upon the health of your conscience.
❑ Take action to resolve any issues you are responsible for—before it's too late.

⊠ Improve health to the best of your ability.

⊠ Use your health to foster goodness.

<u>Notes:</u>

_____

_____

_____

_____

_____

_____

_____

_____

_____

_____

_____

_____

_____

_____

_____

_____

_____

_____

_____

_____

_____

_____

_____

_____

☑ Finding Purpose

☒ Define complete purpose for life:
❑ Reflect on what complete purpose means for you.
❑ Identify and fulfill your needs.
❑ Incorporate goodness into your life to find meaning.

☒ Understand that there is more than a material aspect to life:
❑ Remember, you won't be worrying about material possessions or accomplishments on your deathbed.

☒ Live with goodness by being selfless:
❑ Selfless thoughts and actions, no matter how big or small, are what you will take with you.

☒ Help fulfill your complete purpose by getting back to good:
❑ Have faith.
❑ Connect to goodness.
❑ Be tolerant of the ways in which other people connect.
❑ Be thankful.
❑ Be selfless.
❑ Learn to give.
❑ Take care.
❑ Treat others as you want to be treated.
❑ Be Good.

<u>Notes:</u>

Make Your Difference!

"I cannot believe that the purpose of life is (merely) to be happy. I think the purpose of life is to be useful, to be honorable, to be compassionate. I think it is above all to matter, to count, to stand for something. To have it make some difference that you lived at all."

~Leo Rosten

The ability to make a difference in your life, the life of another person, and the state of our world is always within reach. Find ways you can share: mentor a child, give time and money, show patience with friends and family, sign up as an organ donor, or reach out to offer assistance to those in need.

To assist in bringing more goodness into our world, I have created a non-profit website, www.makeyourdifference.org. You can find hundreds, even thousands of ways to help yourself and others. Here is copy of a press release that explains more about the site..

LAKE VILLA, IL –Maybe solving the world's problems isn't easy; but Ken Ferrara believes pointing out the direction to a solution is.

"The solution is us — all of us — and I aim to show people how they can get involved in making the world a better place," said Ferrara, an Illinois man who is dedicated to positive networking through his web site, MakeYourDifference.Org.

MakeYourDifference.Org is a non-profit site whose name means what it says — providing ways for people make their difference. It is the concrete manifestation of Ferrara's book, *The Goodness Campaign: getting back to good*.

"We've got to get back to doing good," Ferrara said. "We can complain all we want about the environment, poverty, hunger, health, and the state of our world today, but many of those problems can be solved by us. The idea behind Make Your Difference.Org is to inspire, engage, and connect people who realize they can be the solution, with organizations that are up and running, with proven track records at tackling life's problems."

Visitors will find scores of inspirational messages as well as links to charities, organizations and movements dedicated to the common good, that have one thing in common: they want to help.

MakeYourDifference.org includes links to sites to everything from animal rights to environmental issues to improving education and individual health. It includes sections for children and parents, crisis hot lines and links to special needs foundations.

"It's our job here to become a bulls eye for those folks who will learn they can connect to someone interested in solving their problem or, better yet, by helping them solve a problem near and dear to their hearts and those they love," Ferrara said.

Perhaps best of all, MakeYourDifference.Org doesn't put limits on how someone can give something good to the world. Its links include charities, but visitors to the site will find countless ways they can give of their time, in a material manner or spiritually as well.

"We don't concern ourselves with what you want to give or how you want to give it. We just want to help you share it – to get back to doing the good that is in your heart," Ferrara said. "That means there are billions of potential solutions to any one problem, and I'll take those odds any day."

The best way to find yourself,
is to lose yourself in the service to others.

-Gandhi

Please visit MakeYourDifference.org to learn, give, and become inspired. You can find and offer to help in these categories, as well as many more:

- Fight Hunger & Poverty
- Help & Care for Children
- Volunteer!
- Give Your Voice
- Fight Violence & Abuse
- Give Environmentally
- Give Tolerance
- Give and Find Health
- Raise Funds and Awareness
- Faith-Based Giving
- Help Yourself
- Family & Friends
- Give Kindness
- Resources for Parents and Kids
- Care for Animals
- Education
- Give Financially
- Special Needs
- Care
- Hope
- Peace
- Compassion
- Honor Heroes
- Give Forgiveness
- Earn Free Money for Charity
- Sign up for our free newsletter